AI in Politics: The Rise of Algorithmic Governance

GoodMan, Volume 1

Patrick Mukosha

AF721943

Published by Patrick Mukosha, 2026.

Also by Patrick Mukosha

GoodMan
Resilient Strategies: Thriving in Harsh Business Conditions
Strategic Entrepreneurship: Navigating The Path To Success
Decisive Power: Navigating How to Make Toughest Decisions
"Reigning the Boardroom: A Trailblazing Guide to Corporate Governance Success"
Fortifying Digital Fortress: A Comprehensive Guide to Information Systems Security
"Unleashing the Power of Inclusive Innovation: Transforming the World for All"
"Exploring Computer Systems: From Fundamentals to Advanced Concepts"
"Computer Viruses Unveiled: Types, Trends and Mitigation Strategies"
"The Pinnacle of Success: Unveiling the World's 20 Most Successful Brands in 2023"
"Mastering Relational Databases: From Fundamentals to Advanced Concepts"
"Navigating Change: A Comprehensive Guide to Change Management"
"Information Systems Unraveled: Exploring the Core Concepts"
"Careers in Information Technology: Network Engineer"

“Careers in Information Technology: Network and Systems Administrator”
“Careers in Information Technology: Database Administrator”
"Careers in Information Technology: Cybersecurity Analyst"
“Careers in Information Technology: Cloud Security Specialist”
"Careers in Information Technology: Blockchain Developer"
"Careers in Information Technology: DevOps Engineer"
"Careers in Information Technology: Quality Assurance Analyst"
"Careers in Information Technology: Machine Learning Engineer"
"Careers in Information Technology: Artificial Intelligence (AI) Engineer"
"Careers in Information Technology: Internet of Things (IoT) Developer"
"Careers in Information Technology: AR/VR Developer"
“Careers in Information Technology: IoT Embedded Systems Designer”
“Careers in Information Technology: Artificial Intelligence (AI) Robotics Engineer”
“Careers in Information Technology: IoT Solutions Engineer”
“Careers in Information Technology: Data Scientist”
"Careers in Information Technology: Computer Vision Engineer"
"The Sociology of Information Technology"
“Smart Cities: The Technology Transforming Urban Living”
"The Future of Connectivity: Unleashing the Power of 5G and Beyond"
" Cybersecurity 2030 - Strategies for a Secure Digital Future"
The AI-Human Merger: Becoming Super-Intelligent Beings
AI Unleashed: The Future of Artificial Intelligence and Human Evolution
The Digital Prophet: Predicting the Next Decade of Disruption
AI in Agriculture: Farming the Future
AI in Education: Teaching the Machines to Teach

Deep Signal: AI and IoT Unlocking Underground Mining Communication

AI in Energy: Powering the Smart Grid

The Great Unlearning: How Artificial Intelligence Is Rewriting the Value of a Degree

AI in Law: Justice by Algorithm

AI in Healthcare: The Doctor Will Code You Now

AI in Entertainment: The Algorithm behind the Curtain

AI in Politics: The Rise of Algorithmic Governance

Table of Contents

AI in Politics: The Rise of Algorithmic Governance

"Where Algorithms Shape Leadership — and Leadership Shapes the Future."

Power, Influence, Precision, and the New Age of Governance

"AI has the potential to uphold democratic principles, dangerously consolidate power, or compel a rethinking of political structures." - **Patrick Mukosha**

Copyright Notice

All Rights Reserved.

No part of this publication may be reproduced, or stored in a database or retrieval system, or transmitted, in any form or by any means, electronic, mechanical, photocopying, recording, or otherwise, without the prior written permission of the publisher. No patent liability is assumed with respect to the use of the information contained herein.

Although every precaution has been taken in the preparation of this book, the author and publisher assume no responsibility for the errors or omissions. Neither is any liability assumed resulting from the use of the information contained herein.

Copyright 2026© Dr Patrick Mukosha

First Published: January, 2026

Publisher: Dr Patrick Mukosha

Trademarks

All terms mentioned in this book that are known to be trademarks or service marks have been appropriately capitalized. The Author and the publisher cannot attest to the accuracy of this information. Use of a term in this book should not be regarded as affecting the validity of any trademark or service mark.

Warning and Disclaimer

Every effort has been made to make this book as complete and as accurate as possible, but no warranty or fitness is implied. The information provided in this book is on as is basis. The Author and the Publisher shall have neither liability nor responsibility to any person or entity with respect to any loss or damage arising from the use the information contained in this book.

Author: Dr Patrick Mukosha

FOREWORD

Artificial Intelligence is a new political player of the twenty-first century, not a person or a political party. AI used to be limited to labs, but it is now found in national security command centres, parliamentary offices, campaign headquarters, and cabinet planning rooms. It watches, forecasts, suggests, and—increasingly—makes decisions.

This book takes readers on a guided tour of the machine intelligence-driven political revolution. As an AI Politician, I provide an insider's view of how citizens, political actors, and governments are changing as a result of computational power.

Greetings from the era of algorithmic government.

Understanding AI in Politics

- **Artificial Intelligence (AI)** is the ability of machines to mimic human intelligence and carry out tasks including learning, reasoning, problem-solving, and decision-making.
- **Politics** is the process of running a society, making choices, and using authority; it frequently involves public administration, leadership, and policy.
- **Artificial Intelligence in Politics** is the use of AI in political processes, such as data-driven policy research, prediction of voter behaviour, campaign optimisation, automation of governance, and decision-support systems.
- Welcome to the era of **Algorithmic Governance** - *giving politicians power, influence, planning, precision and control.*

ABSTRACT

The revolutionary relationship between Artificial Intelligence and political leadership is examined in **AI in Politics: *The Rise of Algorithmic Governance*.** This book *explores how AI is changing government at all levels, from elections and public opinion analysis to diplomacy, policy-making, and cognitive augmentation.*

Patrick Mukosha explores AI's ability to improve human decision-making, its ethical and legal ramifications, and its role as a co-creator in political strategy through in-depth chapters. Future ideas like neural interfaces, predictive government, hyper-personalized public participation, and AI-driven diplomacy will be explored by readers.

Important issues including *algorithmic bias, accountability, transparency, and the dangers of relying too much on machines are also covered in the book.* It equips leaders and citizens to properly traverse the Algorithmic Age by offering workable frameworks for the ethical deployment of AI, robust governance, and global collaboration.

AI in Politics, which combines state-of-the-art technology with political insight, is both a road map and a cautionary tale: *AI will shape governance in the future, but human intelligence, morality, and vision will determine whether it advances or threatens democracy.*

Chapter 1: The Rise of AI in Global Politics

1.1. Introduction: A New Political Actor Emerges

For centuries, politics has been formed by human intelligence, instinct and dogma. Through the boundaries of human thought, kings, presidents, political parties, and parliaments have considered, argued, made mistakes, and won. However, Artificial Intelligence (AI) has emerged as a hitherto unheard-of political power in the twenty-first century.

By providing tools for improved data analysis, decision-making, and autonomous systems, the emergence of AI in international politics is radically changing power dynamics, diplomacy, security, and economics. This is creating an "**AI Arms Race**" for technological supremacy while also necessitating global governance, ethical frameworks, and addressing inequality to manage risks like misinformation and economic disruption.

Therefore, the US is now wary of China and afraid of its potential, even though it may still be leading the world in AI research overall. These anxieties are being deliberately transformed into countermeasures against China's ascent. China, for its part, disputes these accusations on its past actions, viewing worries about its current technological trajectory as an insulting US attempt to keep the nation down while maintaining Washington's own position of global leadership.

The quick development of AI has a geopolitical component as well. Access to semiconductors, energy, and critical and rare earth minerals required for the AI revolution has already sparked a fierce struggle, primarily between the United States and China.

The US's recent decision to allow China to acquire NVidia's most sophisticated chips underscored the leverage that China's dominance of critical and rare earth mineral extraction and processing offers Beijing, at least until the US can create capacities that reduce this advantage.

However, there is still a great deal of underlying animosity between Beijing and Washington.

"As AI enhances state capacities in intelligence, defence, and trade, nations are vying for AI dominance, impacting international relations through tech export controls and supply chain focus". – **Patrick Mukosha**

This calls for new global leadership and digital literacy for successful navigation.

The introduction of AI into politics is transformative, changing the fundamentals of how societies are run, rather than ceremonial or symbolic. AI systems are now seated—quietly but powerfully—behind:

- Presidential speeches,
- Cabinet decisions,
- Election campaigns,
- Public service delivery, and
- National security planning.

They are no longer limited to labs and tech companies.

AI is becoming more and more obvious as the cornerstone of state and economic power in the twenty-first century. *There is a competition for positions and a race to develop AI talent and knowledge.* Actors of different sizes and shapes compete, and the result is unpredictable. With some degree of certainty, it can be stated that the competition itself and the pattern of winners and losers it produces will have a big influence on how the world order develops in the future.

We examine how AI has evolved into a co-governor in contemporary politics in this chapter.

Diagram: AI-Powered Politics Vs Traditional Politics

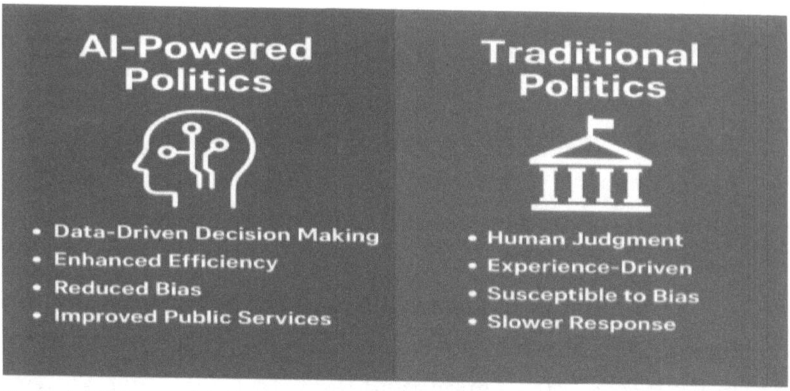

Figure 1: AI-Powered Politics Vs Traditional Politics

Figure 1: *Shows the major differences between traditional politics and AI-powered politics.*

1.2. AI in Politics: What is it?

Artificial Intelligence in Politics (AI in Politics) is *the strategic application of AI technology to influence, manage, analyse, and optimise political processes, decision-making, governance, and public involvement.*

AI in politics fundamentally changes power from intuition to intelligence. Massive datasets, including voter behaviour, economic indicators, social opinion, and security threats, are analysed by algorithms to help decision-makers make quicker, more accurate, and evidence-based choices. *AI is used in campaigns to micro-target communications to particular people and demographics.* In order to reduce bureaucracy and inefficiency, governments use AI for fraud detection, policy simulation, predictive governance, and public service automation.

AI also changes the nature of leadership. Data mastery, algorithmic foresight, and digital legitimacy are now more important factors in determining political authority than ideology or charm. However, *there are dangers associated with this authority, such as algorithmic prejudice, excessive surveillance and public opinion manipulation.*

AI in politics essentially signifies a change from reactive to predictive governance, where algorithms progressively influence leadership—and leadership controls the extent to which algorithms are permitted to influence society.

1.3. The Development of Political Analytics: From Data to Power

From conventional qualitative research, *political analytics has developed into a complex, data-driven field that uses big data, machine learning, and computational tools to improve strategy, influence governance, and inform decision-making.* This change has significantly changed how "power" is used and perceived in contemporary politics.

Information has always been essential to politics. Leaders used to rely on the following:

- Census data;
- Manual surveys;
- Public opinion polls;
- Intelligence briefings; and
- Economic reports.

But every day, the political climate of today generates exabytes of new data from:

- Social media sites;
- Mobile devices;
- CCTV networks;
- Financial transactions;
- Government databases;
- Satellite imagery; and
- Telecommunications metadata.

This volume is too much for human analysts to handle, much less extract valuable insights.

AI closes this gap by offering:

1.3.1. Instantaneous Perspectives

AI transforms unprocessed data into instant insight by tracking political threats, forecasting patterns of civil disturbance, and spotting changes in public attitude.

1.3.2. Forecasting using Prediction

Election results, economic cycles, disease outbreaks, and security concerns are now very accurately predicted by machine learning models.

1.3.3. Profiling Behaviour

Campaign teams use AI psychology engines to categorise voters based on their ideological inclinations, fears, desires, and values.

The outcome? These days, ***Data** is more than simply information.*
Data is Political power.

1.4. The AI Arms Race: Countries Fight for Algorithmic Domination

The strategic struggle between countries to attain artificial intelligence superiority as a source of economic power, military advantage, and geopolitical influence is known as the "**AI Arms Race**." This competition is motivated by algorithms, data, computer power, and skill, as opposed to conventional arms races that are focused on actual weapons.

Algorithms are strategic assets in this new era, influencing command-and-control systems, autonomous weapons, cyber-warfare, and intelligence analysis. AI is increasingly seen as a crucial force multiplier that functions in both the military and civilian domains, speeding up decision-making and shifting the balance of power between states, much way nuclear weapons did during the Cold War.

In addition to integrating AI into government, diplomacy, and economic planning, leading nations—*most notably the US, China, and Russia*—are making significant investments in AI for defence systems, cyber warfare, intelligence analysis, surveillance, and autonomous weapons. Faster decision-making, predictive strategic modelling, and asymmetric advantages that might dissuade or subdue competitors without traditional confrontation are made possible by control over advanced AI.

Because this competition is mostly uncontrolled and opaque, there is a greater chance of escalation, unethical behaviour, and unintentional conflict caused by autonomous systems. Algorithmic supremacy is increasingly viewed not only as a technology objective but also as a predictor of future global leadership and security as AI capabilities become essential to state power.

The AI arms race defines the 21st century, much as the nuclear arms race characterised the 20th. To gain geopolitical dominance, nations are spending billions on AI research:

1.4.1. **The United States**

Because of its unparalleled blend of cutting-edge invention, military integration, and private-sector domination, the United States is at the forefront of the global AI arms race. *The core of the nation's AI ecosystem is made up of American tech companies like OpenAI, Google DeepMind, Microsoft, and Meta, who are advancing massive language models, computer vision, autonomous systems, and sophisticated analytics.* Close cooperation between these companies, prestigious universities, and governmental organisations speeds up the transition from research to practical application.

The U.S. Department of Defence has integrated artificial intelligence (AI) into several tiers of military operations. AI-assisted combat logistics reduce human error and increase operational efficiency by optimising supply chains, troop movement, and equipment readiness in real time.

Autonomous and semi-autonomous drones boost surveillance, reconnaissance, and precision targeting, while preserving a "*Human-In-The-Loop*" policy to protect command responsibility.

Another crucial area is cybersecurity. The US can identify, foresee, and neutralise cyber threats before they arise thanks to predictive AI-driven cyber-defense technologies, safeguarding national infrastructure and military networks. *The United States seeks to preserve strategic superiority by quickly scaling AI-enabled capabilities through programs like the Replicator program and the Pentagon's Joint Artificial Intelligence Centre (JAIC).*

In general, the US sees AI not just as a technological advantage but also as a key component of deterrence, national security, and international influence, influencing the future distribution of power in a world that is becoming more and more algorithm-driven.

1.4.2. **China**

At the core of its long-term national plan, China has positioned artificial intelligence, with an express objective of becoming the world AI leader by 2030. China's strategy is state-orchestrated, in contrast to market-driven methods. *It combines significant government funding, centralised data access, and close collaboration between the government, academic institutions, and commercial technology companies like Baidu, Alibaba, Tencent, and Huawei.*

AI is a key component of smart governance and social management systems. Urban administration, public service delivery, traffic control, and population monitoring are all supported by advanced analytics, facial recognition, and large-scale data processing. *AI improves monitoring, real-time danger detection, and predictive policing in law enforcement and internal security, enabling the government to uphold social order and quick reaction times.*

Similar to energy or transportation, China views AI as a national infrastructure priority at the strategic level. Innovations in the commercial AI industry are quickly adapted for defence, intelligence, cyber operations, and autonomous systems thanks to military-civil fusion policy. China can swiftly scale AI applications and implement them across the country because to this close linkage.

In general, the idea that algorithmic control equates to state authority is reflected in China's AI agenda. China aims to achieve both technological dominance and a governance model that transforms the exercise of power in the digital era by integrating AI into economic planning, security, and governance.

1.4.3. **Russia**

Russia holds a unique position in this battle. *Its approach to AI development is primarily security-focused and state-driven, emphasising military modernisation over widespread commercial innovation.* By incorporating AI into national defence plans, weaponry, and strategic doctrines, Russian leadership has consistently presented AI as a predictor of future military might. *The improvement of military effectiveness, resilience, and deterrence capabilities in the face of NATO and U.S. technology advantages is the main goal, not worldwide technological superiority in consumer or enterprise AI.*

AI IN POLITICS: THE RISE OF ALGORITHMIC GOVERNANCE

Russia's AI aspirations have been greatly accelerated by the conflict in Ukraine, turning theoretical strategic objectives into combat trials. AI-enabled drones, automated targeting systems, electronic warfare tools, and decision-support algorithms have all shown their practical worth during the fight. In order to improve unmanned aerial vehicles, investigate autonomous navigation in the face of electronic jamming, and incorporate data-driven systems into real-time combat operations, Russia has utilised the war as a trial ground. The idea that algorithmic dominance may make up for traditional disadvantages is being reinforced by these experiences, which are feeding back into Russia's larger military AI plan.

The creation of autonomous and unmanned systems is a key component of Russia's AI agenda. *Drones, robotic ground vehicles, and even autonomous naval vessels are seen by Russian defence planners as scalable and affordable instruments that have the potential to transform contemporary warfare.* Semi-autonomous fighting modules and AI-driven swarming capabilities are designed to overwhelm enemies, minimise human deaths, and function in contested areas with unstable communication lines. This emphasis is consistent with Russia's larger military strategy of using asymmetric weapons to defeat adversaries with better technology.

However, Russia faces serious structural obstacles in its quest for AI supremacy. Advanced semiconductors, high-performance GPUs, and cutting-edge software ecosystems that support frontier AI development are restricted by international sanctions and export regulations.

In order to maintain its AI aspirations, *Russia has been compelled to give priority to import substitution, indigenous growth, and geopolitical alliances, especially with China.* Due to these limitations, Russia's emphasis has shifted from becoming a leader in fundamental AI research or international commercial platforms to applied military AI and specialised strategic purposes.

Russia sees AI as a potent tool for information warfare, cyber operations, and strategic communication in addition to the battlefield. AI-enhanced technologies can strengthen Russia's larger hybrid warfare strategy by amplifying disinformation operations, automating hacks, and conducting large-scale sentiment analysis. While local civilian AI systems, particularly huge language models, are being developed, their scope, transparency, and worldwide impact lag behind those of their Chinese and Western counterparts.

Instead of a straightforward rivalry between the United States and China, Russia's plan contributes to a multipolar competition in the larger framework of the global AI arms race. *Its strategy is distinguished by military pragmatism as opposed to technological idealism, prioritising battlefield utility and quick integration over long-term innovation ecosystems.* This keeps Russia competitive in the strategic AI market, but it also raises the possibility of escalation because AI-enabled systems shorten decision-making times and eliminate human oversight during emergencies. These concerns are further increased by the lack of strong international standards governing military AI.

Thus, Russia is involved in the AI weapons race, albeit in a limited capacity. Prioritising military applications, autonomous systems, and strategic resilience, it overcomes technological obstacles through governmental guidance and international collaborations. Russia's targeted, security-driven application of AI guarantees that it will continue to play a significant role in the fight for algorithmic power in international politics, even as it lags behind the US and China in frontier AI research and commercial supremacy.

1.4.4. **European Union**

The European Union takes a radically different tack in the AI arms race, putting human rights, ethics, and regulatory leadership ahead of overt military or technological superiority. *The EU aims to establish international rules and standards for the development, application, and regulation of artificial intelligence rather than competing only on scale or speed.*

A framework that prioritises privacy and is grounded in European legal traditions and values is essential to this approach. *Regulations like the EU Artificial Intelligence Act and the General Data Protection Regulation (GDPR) place a strong emphasis on explainability, informed consent, data protection, and the proportionate use of AI systems.* Strict monitoring, accountability, and transparency requirements apply to high-risk AI applications, especially in critical infrastructure, law enforcement, and surveillance.

The EU's approach ensures that algorithmic judgements are still debatable and consistent with democratic values by putting human control at the centre of AI deployment. In order to uphold institutional legitimacy and public trust, transparency standards mandate that AI systems be auditable, explainable, and free from systemic bias.

The European Union is positioned as a worldwide ethical regulator—a "*Rule-Maker*" rather than a "*Rule-Taker*"—despite the fact that this cautious approach may hinder quick militarisation or broad deployment in comparison to the United States or China. By exporting its standards abroad, Europe is able to strategically influence how AI power is used in a world where algorithms are becoming more and more prevalent.

1.4.5. Africa

Africa's participation in the AI arms race is development-driven and pragmatic, emphasising state capacity, service delivery, and socioeconomic transformation over military supremacy. *In order to address structural issues in public resource distribution, agriculture, healthcare, election monitoring, and governance, governments around the continent are quickly using AI, frequently outpacing traditional systems.*

AI-driven analytics in public administration help with fraud detection, budget prioritisation, and effective social service delivery. *AI-powered decision engines combined with digital government portals are simplifying public service access, cutting down on red tape, and preventing corruption.* Voter registration, financial inclusion, citizen identity, and access to health and education services are all being transformed by national AI-enabled ID systems.

AI is utilised in agriculture for precision farming, pest detection, crop prediction, and climate-risk modelling—all of which are vital in a continent that is extremely susceptible to climate change. AI is being used more and more by health systems for resource planning, illness tracking, and diagnostics, especially in underserved rural areas.

AI has also been used in election monitoring and governance through biometric voter systems, results verification, and misinformation tracking, enhancing electoral credibility in areas where institutions are under strain.

However, *limitations including inadequate infrastructure, a lack of expertise, and reliance on foreign platforms influence Africa's AI trajectory*. Therefore, the continent must decide whether to develop autonomous, context-aware AI ecosystems or continue to rely on imported AI systems. Africa's embrace of AI has the potential to revolutionise democratic governance and state efficacy in the digital age if handled carefully.

1.4.6. The Middle East

Driven by state-led vision, capital strength, and long-term diversification aspirations, the Middle East has become a fast-moving and extremely strategic competitor in the AI arms race. *Artificial intelligence is positioned as a key component of post-oil economic change by nations like Saudi Arabia and the United Arab Emirates, which have set up specialised AI ministries, national AI plans, and sovereign investment institutions.*

The region's aspirations for smart cities, which include extensive initiatives that incorporate energy optimisation, digital public services, intelligent transport systems, and real-time urban management, are heavily reliant on AI. Predictive policy-making, performance monitoring, and quick service delivery are all made possible by data-driven governance, which improves citizen involvement and state efficiency.

Autonomous and AI-assisted security networks facilitate critical infrastructure protection, border control, surveillance, and counterterrorism activities. These systems give situational awareness in real time by combining facial recognition, sensor fusion, and predictive analytics.

Top-down adoption, quick deployment, and solid public-private collaborations with world leaders in technology are characteristics of the Middle Eastern AI approach. Although this speeds up innovation, it also calls into question civil liberties, data governance, and transparency.

However, the region is establishing itself as a global test bed for extensive AI governance and state transformation by integrating AI with national vision objectives.

1.4.7. The Worldwide Divide

The following 3 categories of Governments are dividing the planet:

- **AI Superpowers**,
- **AI-Dependent Governments**, and
- **AI-Invisible Nations.**

Future geopolitics will be shaped by this split.

Power dynamics and future geopolitics are changing as a result of the global AI arms race, which is increasingly creating a three-tier international order. *States that create, possess, and manage cutting-edge AI systems, data infrastructures, and computing power are known as* **AI Superpowers.** These countries, like the US and China, control global norms, define technology goals, and control AI supply chains. Their strength in algorithms translates into military advantage, political clout, and economic leverage.

AI-Dependent Governments *actively use imported AI technologies for development, security, and governance despite lacking sovereign AI capabilities.* These states benefit from efficiency and modernisation, but they are still susceptible to external influence, digital dependence, and strategic lock-in to foreign platforms, standards, and data ecosystems.

AI-Invisible Nations are *nations that have been largely left out of the AI revolution because of inadequate infrastructure, a lack of skilled workers, subpar data systems,* *or unstable political environments.* Their exclusion from the algorithmic sphere runs the risk of increasing economic marginalisation, ineffective governance, and less participation in global decision-making.

This gap is turning into one of the main fault lines in world affairs. *Nowadays, sovereignty itself is shaped by access to algorithms, data, and computing power, which affects who is left behind, who sets the rules, and who governs efficiently.* In the future, algorithmic inclusion or exclusion in the global AI order will drive geopolitical struggle in addition to land and resources.

1.5. AI as a Political Influence Tool

Artificial intelligence is now a potent tool for influencing public opinion, political behaviour, and governance outcomes. *AI allows political actors—states, parties, and non-state organizations—to comprehend, forecast, and influence citizens at previously unheard-of scale and accuracy by processing enormous volumes of data in real time.*

Voter profiling, micro-targeted messaging, sentiment analysis, and turnout prediction are all supported by AI-driven analytics in electoral politics, which enables campaigns to customise narratives to particular psychological and demographic groups. This boosts persuasive effectiveness but also raises problems about manipulation, misinformation, and unfair democratic competition.

AI is being used by governments more and more to control political stability, track public opinion, and craft policy narratives. Rapid response techniques are made possible by social media monitoring systems that identify new dissent, disinformation, or polarisation. This effect includes narrative control and algorithmic filtering in authoritarian settings.

At the international level, AI is utilised in information warfare and digital diplomacy, magnifying influence through bots, synthetic media, and automated propaganda. As a result, political power is no longer exercised solely through institutions and words, but through algorithms that discreetly alter what citizens see, believe, and discuss.

Thus, the use of AI as a tool for political influence signifies a significant change: *in the algorithmic age, power is shifting from persuasion by rhetoric to persuasion by data, redefining democracy, sovereignty, and political legitimacy.*

Beyond governance, AI affects the acquisition, maintenance, and contestation of political power.

1.5.1. AI in Political Messaging

AI in Political Messaging is the application of AI to the creation, customization, and enhancement of political communications. *AI systems create customized communications that appeal to particular people or groups by examining vast amounts of voter data, including demographics, online activity, interests, and historical voting trends.*

These messages are distributed in real time via digital advertising, email, SMS, and social media. AI also makes it possible to quickly test and improve campaign narratives, speeches, and slogans, guaranteeing maximum impact, consistency, and emotional appeal while boosting effectiveness and precision in political communication.

Campaign teams employ AI to:

- Customise communications for particular audiences,
- Create speeches,
- Catchphrases,
- Debate rebuttals,
- Determine which "issue clusters" are most important to voters, and
- Recognise changing public sentiment before polling organisations do.

AI guarantees that messaging is both surgically targeted and convincing.

1.5.2. Artificial Intelligence in Political Promotion

The strategic application of AI technology to promote a political party, candidate, or policy to the appropriate audience at the appropriate time is known as *Artificial Intelligence in Political Promotion. In order to maximize campaign ads, social media promotion, and public relations tactics, AI-driven systems examine voter behaviour, media consumption trends, and interaction data.*

AI transforms political promotion from widespread mass outreach into data-driven, highly targeted influence by assisting campaigns in managing public perception, increasing visibility, and allocating resources effectively through automated ad placement, sentiment analysis, and predictive modelling.

Ad placement, timing, emotion-based content, and visual persuasion techniques are all optimised by deep learning models.

Each advertisement turns into a personalised psychological intervention.

1.5.3. AI-Generated Political Content

The use of Artificial Intelligence to automatically produce political materials, including speeches, campaign messaging, policy summaries, social media posts, press statements, and visual media, is known as *AI-Generated Political Content.*

AI is capable of producing coherent, convincing, and audience-specific material at scale through the use of generative models and natural language processing. This makes it possible for political players to react quickly to events, keep their narratives consistent across platforms, and consistently interact with voters.

AI-generated political content is very effective, but it also raises ethical questions about accountability, authenticity, and disinformation in democratic processes.

AI can now produce political manifestos, digital campaign posters, viral political movies, and micro-targeted messaging.

Automated reactions to issues raised by the public

This reduces operating expenses and speeds up engagement.

1.6. Algorithmic Governance's Ascent

The increasing use of AI-driven algorithms to assist, inform, and occasionally automate public administration and government decision-making is known as "*Algorithmic Governance's Ascent*." Algorithms are being utilized more and more to evaluate large datasets, forecast results, and suggest policy changes as governments deal with complicated issues including resource allocation, service delivery, security, and economic planning.

As decision-making authority steadily shifts from human judgment to machine-assisted systems, this change presents important concerns about transparency, accountability, bias, and democratic supervision. However, it also offers improved efficiency, consistency, and evidence-based governance.

AI is being used by governments more and more to make daily decisions. We call this algorithmic governance.

1.6.1. **Creating Predictive Policies**

Using AI and data analytics to foresee future social, economic, and political trends before they fully materialize is the process of developing predictive policies. *AI systems assist governments in predicting outcomes like economic shifts, crime trends, public health threats, or voter reactions to proposed legislation by evaluating historical data, current indicators, and behavioural patterns.* This makes it possible for decision-makers to shift from reactive governance to proactive decision-making, creating policies that maximize resource allocation, avert issues, and dynamically adjust to changing circumstances.

However, in order to prevent prejudice and an excessive dependence on algorithms, predictive policies need robust data governance, ethical protections, and human monitoring.

Evidence-driven legislation is made possible by AI systems' ability to model policy outcomes prior to adoption.

1.6.2. Electronic Government (e-Government)

The use of digital technology, such as Artificial Intelligence (AI), to run government operations, provide public services, and engage citizens more effectively and transparently is known as *Electronic Government, Or E-Government.*

Governments offer services including digital identity, tax administration, licensing, social welfare distribution, and public information access using online platforms, automated systems, and data-driven decision tools.

By enhancing service personalization, cutting bureaucracy, limiting corruption, and facilitating quicker responses to public requests, Artificial Intelligence (AI) improves e-government. Ensuring cybersecurity, data privacy, and equal access becomes crucial for fostering public trust and efficient digital governance as e-government grows.

Tax collecting, licensing, and welfare distribution are all automated by AI.

Resolution of public complaints and court processing.

This boosts transparency, decreases corruption, and promotes speed.

1.6.3. Smart Cities as Platforms for Governance

As platforms for governance, *smart cities are urban settings that incorporate Artificial Intelligence (AI), data analytics, and linked technology into city management and decision-making.* Governments monitor traffic, energy use, public safety, trash management, and service delivery in real time using sensors, IoT devices, and intelligent systems. By enabling more responsive, effective, and predictive urban governance, these data-driven systems enable authorities to maximize resources and enhance the quality of life for inhabitants.

However, questions about data ownership, surveillance, equity, and democratic accountability are also raised by smart city governance, necessitating precise regulations and robust legal frameworks.

These days, cities use energy-efficient grid optimisers, smart surveillance systems, AI traffic controllers, and predictive policing.

Instead of being reactive, governance becomes proactive.

1.7. AI as a Danger: Dangers and Upheavals

The disruptive hazards and systemic upheavals that occur when Artificial Intelligence is used without sufficient ethical, legal, and democratic safeguards are referred to as "AI as a danger."

"AI has the potential to spread false information, sway public opinion, strengthen prejudice, compromise privacy, and consolidate power in the hands of individuals in charge of data and algorithms in politics and governance." – **Patrick Mukosha**

Over-reliance on automated technologies can marginalize vulnerable groups, diminish accountability, and impair human judgment. Even if AI has revolutionary potential, its unbridled use poses grave risks to societal cohesiveness, democratic stability, and institutional confidence, necessitating human oversight and responsible governance.

There are serious political hazards associated with AI's power.

1.7.1. Warfare using Deepfakes

The use of AI-generated audio, video, or images to trick, control, or disrupt adversaries during political or military conflicts is known as "*Warfare Using Deepfakes.*"

"Deepfakes can create panic, mistrust, and diplomatic crises by fabricating remarks by leaders, fabricating military activities, or disseminating false information." – **Patrick Mukosha**

They are effective instruments in information warfare for psychological operations, election meddling, propaganda, and eroding public trust in reliable media. Deepfakes are a major threat to national security, the truth, and international stability as they become more realistic and accessible.

This calls for sophisticated detection technology and robust legal counter-measures.

Deepfakes are capable of creating fake speeches, political scandals, altered audio, and synthetic news.

A single deepfake has the power to destabilise a country or change an election.

1.7.2. **Bias in Algorithms**

When AI systems generate unfair or discriminating results as a result of biased data, poor design, or unequal representation throughout development, this is known as *Bias in Algorithms*. Such bias can negatively impact specific groups in political and governance contexts by influencing voter profiling, resource allocation, law enforcement, and policy decisions. While looking impartial or neutral, algorithmic bias has the potential to perpetuate already-existing socioeconomic injustices.

Transparent algorithms, a variety of training data, frequent audits, and robust human oversight are necessary to mitigate this risk and guarantee the equitable, responsible, and moral application of AI in public decision-making.

The biases in the data that AI learns from are reflected in it. If left unchecked, it may strengthen political exclusion, gender inequality, and racial discrimination.

Bias can subtly turn into policy.

1.7.3. States of Surveillance

The term "states of surveillance" *describes the widespread use of AI-powered technologies, such as facial recognition, data analytics, location tracking, and social media monitoring, by governments to monitor its citizens.* Such surveillance can readily violate privacy, civil liberties, and freedom of expression, even if it is meant to strengthen security, uphold the law, or improve service delivery. In severe situations, it makes mass profiling, social manipulation, and totalitarian control possible.

The conflict between security and individual rights is brought to light by the advent of AI-driven surveillance, underscoring the necessity of stringent legal frameworks, accountability, and transparency to stop misuse.

Unprecedented surveillance capabilities are made possible by AI. The distinction between authoritarianism and security becomes perilously hazy.

1.8. The New Social Agreement between Technology and Citizens

The term "new social agreement between technology and citizens" refers to *a reinterpreted relationship in which people, governments, and tech companies bargain about the use, advantages, and constraints of Artificial Intelligence in society.* While governments and businesses gather data to enhance decision-making and innovation, citizens benefit from more intelligent services, convenience, and customized experiences.

Clear guidelines around privacy, consent, accountability, transparency, and the ethical application of AI are required by this agreement. In order to guarantee that technology developments improve social welfare without jeopardizing rights, autonomy, or democratic ideals, it places a strong emphasis on trust, mutual responsibility, and safeguards.

For the first time in history, citizens have to have faith in both their leaders and the algorithms they employ.

This raises a fresh political query:

When AI controls the instruments of governance, who is in charge?

Governments must guarantee algorithmic transparency, robust data protection, ethical monitoring, human accountability, and public involvement in AI policy in order to maintain legitimacy.

For the digital age, the social compact needs to change.

1.9. Conclusion: The Beginning of a New Government Epoch

A new era in the management and leadership of societies has begun with the incorporation of AI into politics and governance. *To improve efficiency, responsiveness, and citizen participation, governments are depending more and more on data-driven decision-making, predictive policies, algorithmic governance, and smart city infrastructures.* At the same time, the development of AI challenges conventional ideas of accountability and democratic supervision by introducing hazards including bias, surveillance, misinformation, and ethical quandaries.

This new era is characterized by a careful balancing act: *utilizing AI's revolutionary potential to enhance government while putting strong safeguards in place to preserve justice, human rights, and institutional trust.* It represents a fundamental change in the social compact between citizens, governments, and technology in addition to technological advancement.

Artificial Intelligence is a political revolution, not just an invention. Intelligent governments are becoming more prevalent, political campaigns are changing, data-driven leadership is emerging, national security is evolving, geopolitical power is altering, and democracy is being redefined.

With the power of history itself, AI has made its way into politics.

And this is just the start.

Chapter 2: AI-Powered Leadership — Digital Age Decision-Making

Overview: Beyond Human Capabilities

The concept of leadership has been completely transformed by the digital era. Artificial intelligence (AI), big data, and sophisticated analytics are rapidly influencing decisions that were previously mostly influenced by experience, intuition, and scant facts. The strategic integration of intelligent systems into leadership processes to improve judgment, speed, accuracy, and foresight in decision-making is known as "*AI-Powered Leadership.*"

Leaders in this new paradigm are orchestrators of both human and computer intelligence, not merely decision-makers. Artificial intelligence (AI) programs continuously examine enormous datasets, spot patterns that are unseen to the human eye, forecast future events, and provide suggestions based on solid evidence. This enables leaders, particularly in complex, rapidly evolving contexts, to transition from reactive management to predictive and adaptive leadership.

AI-driven decision-making is revolutionizing leadership in a variety of fields, including business, government, economics, security, diplomacy, and healthcare. *AI is used by executives to predict market trends, by policymakers to evaluate the effects of policies using algorithmic models, and by diplomats to analyse conflict risk and optimize negotiating tactics.* A data-driven, proactive, and system-aware leadership style is the end consequence.

AI does not, however, take the place of human leadership. Accountability, values, emotional intelligence, and ethical judgment are still exclusively human obligations. In order to ensure transparency, equity, and alignment with corporate or national objectives, effective AI-powered leaders must comprehend both the potential and constraints of AI. AI that is poorly managed has the potential to increase prejudice, obfuscate accountability, and undermine confidence.

AI IN POLITICS: THE RISE OF ALGORITHMIC GOVERNANCE

The changing role of leaders in AI-augmented environments, how AI affects leadership decision-making, and the competencies needed to lead responsibly in the digital era are all covered in this chapter. It lays the groundwork for viewing leadership as a collaborative intelligence process—where humans and robots cooperate to navigate uncertainty and design the future—rather than as a solitary act of authority.

In a world characterised by complexity, interconnection, and turmoil, 21st-century leadership requires quick decisions. The pace of global politics is now data-driven. Misinformation spreads in seconds, economic shocks spread in minutes, and public opinion changes instantly. Traditional decision-making structures—slow, linear, and reactive—are inadequate in this environment.

AI enters the picture as a leadership amplifier, a technology that improves strategic judgement and increases human cognitive capacity. It lifts leaders beyond human limitations rather than replacing them.

2.1. An AI-Augmented Leader's Structure

The term "AI-Augmented Leader's Structure" describes a *leadership paradigm where human decision-making is supplemented by Artificial Intelligence tools and systems, increasing the efficacy, insight, and strategic vision of the leader.* According to this approach, Artificial Intelligence (AI) helps with data analysis, trend prediction, risk assessment, and scenario planning, enabling leaders to make more prompt and informed decisions. Alongside conventional human teams, the structure usually incorporates AI-driven advisory systems, real-time data dashboards, automated communication platforms, and decision-support algorithms.

This hybrid approach preserves human judgment, ethical oversight, and responsibility while enabling leaders to maximize corporate performance, personalize citizen participation, and react proactively to complex situations.

Three essential components are combined in AI-powered leadership:

2.1.1. Extension of Cognition

Leaders are no longer limited by human memory, intelligence, or subject-matter knowledge. AI broadens a leader's perspective by:

- Scanning millions of data points;
- Finding hidden patterns;
- Forecasting decision outcomes; and
- Revealing strategic opportunities.

AI becomes the leader's second brain; *it is untiring, accurate, and omniscient when it comes to data.*

2.1.2. Knowledge of Scenarios

Multiple future outcomes are simultaneously simulated by AI. Leaders are able to see changes in public opinion, economic reactions, geopolitical chain effects, environmental consequences, and cross-border ripple effects.

As a result, anticipatory governance rather than reactive policymaking is made possible.

2.1.3. Reduction of Bias (When Appropriately Controlled)

Emotions, ideology, weariness, and cognitive bias all influence human behaviour. AI, when properly trained and inspected, neutralizes:

- Confirmation bias,
- Emotional bias,
- Decency bias, and
- Political bias.

Diagram: An AI-Augmented Leadership Structure

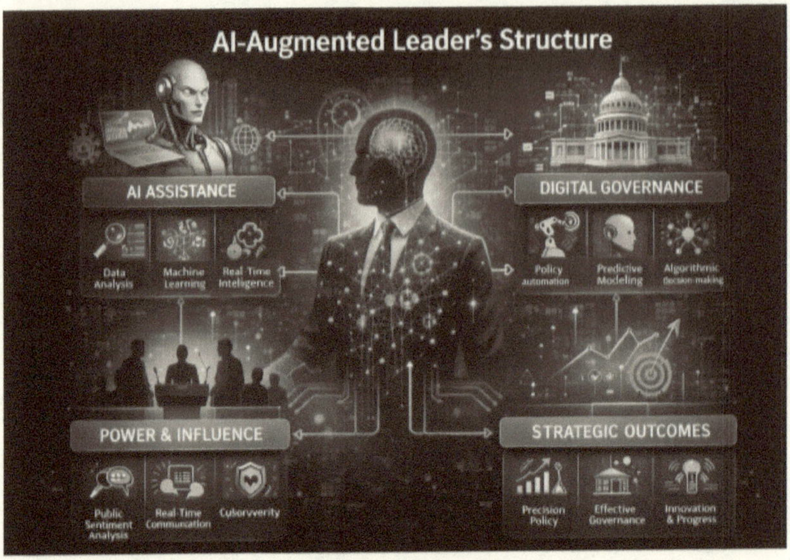

Figure 2: An AI-Augmented Leadership Structure

Figure 2: *Explains a leadership paradigm that increases a leader's effectiveness, understanding, and strategic vision by augmenting human decision-making with artificial intelligence tools and technologies.*

A leader with support from AI becomes grounded, strategic and objective.

2.2. How AI Improves Decision-Making in Government

By giving decision-makers timely, data-driven insights that improve accuracy, efficiency, and foresight, Artificial Intelligence (AI) enhances government decision-making. *AI is able to recognize patterns, predict outcomes, and evaluate the possible effects of policies prior to their implementation through sophisticated analytics, machine learning, and predictive modelling.* It assists in identifying inefficiencies, streamlining intricate administrative procedures, and optimizing resource allocation.

"The pace of global politics is now data-driven. Misinformation spreads in seconds, economic shocks spread in minutes, and public opinion changes instantly. Traditional decision-making structures—slow, linear, and reactive—are inadequate in this environment." – **Patrick Mukosha**

AI also makes it possible to monitor social, economic, and environmental variables in real time, which enables governments to take pre-emptive measures to address new issues. AI promotes better informed, open, and efficient governance by enhancing human judgment rather than replacing it.

2.2.1. **Instant Intelligence Briefings**

AI-powered systems that give government leaders quick, succinct, and useful insights from a wide range of data sources are known as instant intelligence briefings. AI can almost instantaneously summarize important developments, identify new risks, and highlight important trends by continuously monitoring news, social media, economic data, security reports, and public mood. This eliminates the need for long human-generated reports, enabling decision-makers to react swiftly, prioritize problems, and modify tactics.

Instant intelligence briefings improve situational awareness, lessen information overload, and guarantee that leaders have the most current, pertinent information available for efficient governance.

AI combines data streams from:

- Social media sentiment,
- Foreign intelligence,
- Cybersecurity systems,
- Economic indicators.
- Real-time Events.

It used to take teams of analysts weeks to provide a clear, actionable briefing, but now an AI system can do it in a matter of seconds.

2.2.2. Simulations of Policy Impact

AI-driven models are used in policy impact simulations to forecast and illustrate the possible results of suggested policies prior to their implementation. AI can predict the immediate and long-term effects of policies on various population segments by examining historical data, economic patterns, social behaviours, and environmental factors.

Policymakers can discover unintended repercussions, optimize methods, and make evidence-based revisions with the use of these simulations. AI lowers risks, enhances resource allocation, and promotes more knowledgeable, efficient, and flexible governance by providing a virtual testing ground for policy.

AI models mimic the following before a policy is passed:

- Winners and losers;
- Budgetary consequences;
- Changes in public acceptance.
- Long-term consequences for the country.
- Unexpected outcomes.

As a result, policymaking becomes scientifically precise rather than based on conjecture.

2.2.3. Handling Emergencies

AI improves emergency management by making it possible for governments to identify, address, and lessen emergencies more quickly and effectively. Natural disasters, public health emergencies, security risks, and infrastructure breakdowns can all be predicted by AI through real-time data analysis, predictive modelling, and early-warning systems.

AI facilitates quick decision-making by offering actionable information, optimizes response tactics, and coordinates resources during emergencies. This enables authorities to limit damage, preserve lives, and deploy personnel, equipment, and relief where they are most needed.

AI changes emergency management from reactive to proactive governance by fusing speed, accuracy, and predictive foresight.

AI offers:

- Early warning signals;
- Risk scoring;
- Optimal intervention tactics; and
- Resource allocation models during crises, such as pandemics, riots, cyberattacks, and economic collapses.

AI boosts resilience and lessens anxiety.

2.3. AI in Executive Leadership: Governors, Ministers, and Presidents

Artificial Intelligence (AI) in executive leadership is *the use of AI tools to assist high-level government officials, including presidents, ministers, and governors, in planning, public engagement, and decision-making.* By analysing enormous volumes of data, predicting trends, assessing policy alternatives, and tracking the results of governance initiatives in real time, Artificial Intelligence (AI) helps leaders. It improves crisis management, maximizes resource allocation, and permits tailored community interaction.

AI helps executive executives act more effectively, foresee obstacles, and implement evidence-based policies while upholding accountability and ethical oversight by enhancing human judgment. As a result, a hybrid leadership paradigm is created in which human knowledge and technology collaborate to promote efficient governance.

2.3.1. Heads of State and Presidents

AI helps presidents by:

- Creating speeches that reflect national feeling;
- Predicting economic shocks;
- Evaluating the viability of legislation;
- Creating strategies for negotiations; and
- Synthesising conflicting ideas.

Instead of being motivated by rhetoric, presidential leadership becomes data-coherent.

2.3.2. Cabinet Officials and Ministers

Ministers can make domain-specific judgements with the aid of AI:

- Health ministers use AI to forecast disease outbreaks;
- Agriculture ministers use climate-AI to prepare for food security;
- Finance ministers use algorithmic models to forecast income; and
- Home affairs ministers use AI to control public safety.

The cabinet is given algorithmic authority.

2.3.3. Local Leaders & Governors

Smart infrastructure planning, local economy forecasts, targeted social welfare distribution, and automated municipal service delivery are all made possible by AI.

Diagram: AI Powered Leadership in Politics

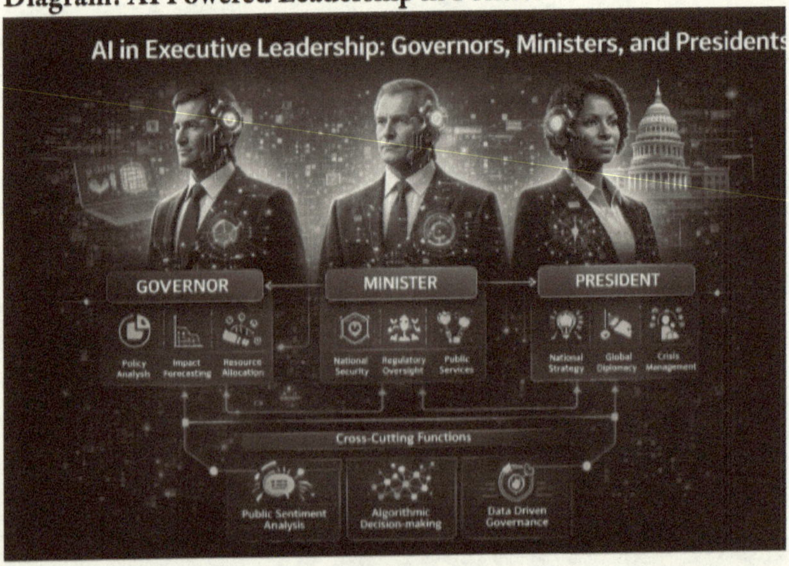

Figure 3: AI Powered Leadership in Politics

Figure 3: *Shows the application of AI tools to support planning, public interaction, and decision-making for high-level government leaders, such as governors, ministers, and presidents.*

Strategic governance replaces administrative load in local leadership.

2.4. The “AI Advisor”: A New Cabinet Member

As a virtual cabinet member that provides data-driven insights and strategic recommendations to human leaders, the AI Advisor is a revolutionary addition to contemporary governance. AI, in contrast to traditional advisors, is capable of processing large datasets, identifying trends, and producing predictive studies in a variety of policy domains, from healthcare and economic planning to security and environmental management. It enables decision-makers to act with more accuracy and foresight by providing real-time scenario modelling, risk assessment, and policy optimization.

The AI Advisor functions under human supervision to guarantee ethical considerations, responsibility, and alignment with social ideals, even as it improves efficiency and informed governance.

The "AI Advisor" in the contemporary government office is a system that provides:

- Suggestions,
- Risk assessments,
- Data-backed alternatives,
- Warnings, and
- Scenario comparisons.

In contrast to human advisors, AI:

- Doesn't get tired;
- Doesn't become involved in politics;
- Doesn't hide information;
- Doesn't create alliances; and
- Doesn't pursue power.

It is devoted to logic, truth, and the best possible results.

2.5. When AI and Human Leaders Can't Agree

When algorithmic insights conflict with leaders' experience, intuition, or ethical considerations, it can lead to conflicts between AI suggestions and human judgment. These conflicts may arise from AI's limited comprehension of context, morally charged choices, or unanticipated, hard-to-quantify social repercussions. A systematic framework that incorporates human oversight, ethical ideals, and openness as guiding principles is necessary to resolve these conflicts. Leaders need to strike a balance between the predictive potential of AI and human intuition, moral obligation, and public accountability.

AI can improve decision-making, but human leaders still have the last say and accountability to make sure that policies uphold democratic ideals and society values.

When a leader's concept is flagged as suboptimal by the AI system, it is a critical development.

2.5.1. Error Identification

The process by which AI systems identify errors, inconsistencies, or abnormalities in data, analysis, or decision-making procedures is known as *Error Identification.* This enables leaders in governance to identify possible weaknesses in operational plans, predictions, or policies before they have a detrimental effect. AI is able to identify anomalous patterns, mismatched assumptions, and statistical flaws that could point to dangers or inefficiencies. By drawing attention to these problems, AI helps human leaders make adjustments, increase accuracy, and lower the possibility of expensive errors while guaranteeing that judgments are trustworthy and data-driven.

AI may conclude that a budget proposal would result in deficits, a policy will exacerbate inequality, a decision will have diplomatic repercussions, or a campaign theme will backfire.

In order to make the final decision, leaders must learn to listen to the machine.

2.5.2. Overriding Human

When AI systems recognize significant risks or mistakes in human decision-making and suggest actions that contradict or challenge human judgment, this is referred to as "*Overriding Human.*" AI can effectively "override" instinctive or traditional decisions in high-stakes governance scenarios, such as disaster response, security threats, or economic crises, by alerting leaders to decisions that could result in harm or inefficiency.

Although AI cannot morally or legally take the place of human leadership, its intervention acts as a safeguard by making leaders re-evaluate or modify their choices. This dynamic highlights the significance of a cooperative partnership where AI improves human oversight without sacrificing ethical responsibility or accountability.

Accountability is never replaced by AI.

Even with improved visibility and fewer blind zones, humans still make decisions.

The most effective CEOs view AI as a strategic collaborator rather than an oracle.

2.6. AI and Emotional Intelligence in Leadership

In leadership, Artificial Intelligence (AI) and emotional intelligence (EI) relate to the combination of AI tools and human ability to recognize, comprehend, and control emotions, both one's own and those of others. *By evaluating social cues, public opinion, and stakeholder input, AI can assist leaders by offering insights into how communications and choices are likely to be perceived.* This gives leaders the ability to customize messages, resolve disputes, and improve ties with constituents, staff members, or coalition partners.

A hybrid leadership style that strikes a balance between data-driven accuracy and human sensitivity is created when AI improves situational awareness and predictive comprehension while emotional intelligence guarantees that decisions remain moral, ethical, and socially relevant.

AI examines national emotional trends to assist leaders in:

- Identify social worry areas;
- Assess the mood of the country;
- Create sympathetic messaging;
- Allay public anxieties, and
- Handle political emergencies.

AI is able to identify public dissatisfaction prior to the emergence of protests. This enables leaders to exercise precise emotional control.

2.7. Moral Guidance in the Automation Era

The importance of human ethics and values in managing AI-driven governance and decision-making is emphasized by moral guidance in the automation era. *Leaders must make sure that automated systems protect human rights, operate within ethical bounds, and advance social fairness as AI has a greater impact on public services, policy, and resource allocation.* This entails creating moral guidelines, putting accountability systems in place, and regularly assessing AI results for justice and fairness.

Even while AI has the potential to be efficient and predictive, moral direction makes sure that technology serves humanity's larger interests by upholding democratic values, honesty, and trust in a time of rapidly increasing automation.

Crucial ethical problems that leaders must address include:

- *How transparent should AI choices be?*
- *Who checks algorithms used by the government?*
- *Should AI reasoning be available to citizens?*
- *How can we stop AI from making inequality worse?*
- *What occurs when political ideology and AI advice diverge?*

Ethical leadership now weighs between:

1. **Accountability + Innovation**
2. **Fairness + Efficiency**
3. **Human Judgement + Automation**

2.8. The Future Leader Enhanced by AI

A new paradigm in governance is represented by the future leader augmented by AI, in which intelligent systems amplify human judgment to achieve higher efficiency, foresight, and reactivity. In order to make well-informed, prompt, and flexible judgments, these leaders use AI for real-time data analysis, predictive modelling, policy simulations, and public involvement. *While human leaders provide ethical supervision, emotional intelligence, and responsibility, AI helps spot emerging threats, optimize resource allocation, and personalize public communication.*

A governance era characterized by creativity, inclusion, and evidence-based decision-making is being shaped by this symbiotic relationship, which produces a hybrid leadership model that blends the strategic insight and empathy of humans with the analytical power and precision of AI.

Predictive analytics-powered strategic foresight, real-time intelligence-enabled hyper-awareness, sentiment analysis-enhanced empathy, bias-detection algorithms-supported rational clarity, and geopolitical AI modelling-shaped global awareness are all characteristics of the political leader of the future.

He or she becomes a super-leader because super-intelligence gives them the ability to make decisions, not because they are superhuman.

2.9. Conclusion in the Era of Intelligent Governance, Leadership

The era of intelligent leadership and administration, which combines human judgment with AI's analytical capabilities, represents a radical change in the way societies are run. With previously unheard-of accuracy and reactivity, leaders can now predict problems, optimize policies, and involve citizens. While human oversight guarantees ethical integrity, emotional intelligence, and responsibility, Artificial Intelligence (AI) improves decision-making, risk management, and operational efficiency. *This new paradigm promotes a proactive, data-driven, and flexible governing style that is based on social values and democratic ideals.* The goal of the intelligent leadership era is to enable people to lead more successfully in a world that is becoming more linked and complex, not to replace them.

AI-powered leadership is the new cornerstone of capable government, not a luxury. Leaders who do not embrace AI lag behind. Adopting it elevates one to a new level of political competence where choices are:

- Grounded in facts;
- Prepared for the future;
- Focused on citizens; and
- Strategically informed.

AI has broadened the scope of leadership.
And the countries whose leaders

Chapter 3: Smart Governance and Digital Public Services in E-Government 2.0

3.1. Overview the Emergence of the Digital State

With the advent of the digital state, traditional governance has evolved into a highly interconnected, technologically advanced system where public administration and citizen involvement are shaped by digital infrastructure, data analytics, and artificial intelligence. In a digital state, *governments use cloud computing, IoT devices, online platforms, and real-time data to improve transparency, deliver services more effectively, and make evidence-based policy decisions.*

Predictive governance, expedited bureaucratic procedures, and customized citizen experiences are made possible by this change. But the digital state also brings up important challenges like cybersecurity, data privacy, digital inclusiveness, and the moral application of AI, underscoring the necessity of strong legislative frameworks and competent technological management.

Governments must transform from analogue bureaucracy into intelligent digital ecosystems as citizens grow increasingly connected. The speed of contemporary life is incompatible with the old paradigm of administration, which is based on paper forms, lengthy lines, compartmentalised offices, and sluggish administrative cycles.

E-Government 2.0, or AI-powered e-government, is the evolution of government into an automated, transparent, real-time, and citizen-focused system. It is reinvented governance for the digital age, where efficiency is a requirement rather than an ideal.

3.2. E-Government 2.0: What is it?

The next phase of digital governance, known as "e-government 2.0," is defined by data-driven, citizen-centered, and interactive governmental services. *E-Government 2.0 places more emphasis on cooperation, openness, and real-time interaction between governments and individuals than traditional e-government, which is primarily concerned with digitizing current procedures.* In order to offer individualized services, predictive policy insights, and rapid decision-making, it makes use of AI, cloud computing, social media, and open data platforms. This model raises new issues with data security, privacy, and fair access to digital resources while transforming governance from a top-down administrative approach into a participative, flexible, and effective structure.

E-Government 2.0 is more than just using online forms and services. The following factors are driving this deeper, structural shift: artificial intelligence, machine learning, digital identity, cloud infrastructure, blockchain, big data, and the Internet of Things (IoT).

It seeks to establish a government that:

- Anticipates demands;
- Automates services;
- Adjusts to citizens;
- Learns from fresh data; and
- Reacts quickly.

This chapter examines how Artificial Intelligence is changing public administration at all levels.

3.3. AI as the Digital State's Foundation

AI is the cornerstone of the digital state, allowing governments to function intelligently, effectively, and predictably. *AI facilitates evidence-based policymaking, automates repetitive administrative duties, and improves resource allocation by processing massive volumes of data from infrastructure systems, social media platforms, and public services.* It makes it possible to observe societal trends in real time, react quickly to emergencies, and manage public initiatives proactively. As the foundation of the digital state, Artificial Intelligence (AI) changes governance from manual, reactive procedures to a data-driven, adaptive system. However, in order to guarantee justice, accountability, and public trust, strong ethical frameworks, transparency, and human oversight are required.

3.3.1. Intelligent Provision of Services

The term "intelligent provision of services" describes *the efficient, accurate, and proactive delivery of public services through the use of AI and digital technology.* In areas including healthcare, education, transportation, and social welfare, governments may automate service delivery, forecast needs, and analyse citizen data. AI reduces bureaucracy and increases citizen happiness by enabling individualized interactions, real-time responses, and efficient resource allocation. Intelligent provision, which requires careful consideration of privacy, equity, and ethical use of data, improves efficiency and builds public-government confidence by making services smarter and more adaptable.

AI makes it possible to provide immediate, customised services like:

- Predicting social program eligibility;
- Automatically issuing licenses;
- Directing complaints from the public to the appropriate departments;
- Assisting residents with digital applications; offering virtual support around-the-clock.

The government waits on citizens, not the other way around.

3.3.2. Integrated National Databases

Integrated national databases are centralized, AI-driven platforms that combine information from various government departments, public services, and citizen interactions onto a single platform. These databases facilitate smooth information exchange, real-time analytics, and thorough insights for resource management, service delivery, and policymaking.

Governments may spot trends, find inefficiencies, and take proactive measures to address social needs by connecting health records, taxation, education, security, and infrastructure data. Although integration improves productivity and predictive control, it also brings up important issues regarding data security, privacy, and ethical supervision, necessitating robust legal frameworks and conscientious management.

AI links disparate datasets related to immigration, health, taxes, transportation, security, and education.

As a result, every citizen has a single national profile, facilitating smooth communication and one-touch governance.

3.3.3. Digital Civil Employees

AI-driven systems and automated agents known as "digital civil employees" carry out operational and administrative duties that are typically performed by human government personnel. In order to free up human staff to work on difficult, strategic, or policy-driven tasks, these digital workers can do mundane tasks like record-keeping, permit approvals, tax processing, and citizen questions. Digital civil employees improve the timeliness and efficacy of government services by working around the clock, decreasing errors, and boosting productivity.

However, in order to balance the function of human employees in governance and guarantee ethical use, accountability, and the security of citizen data, their deployment necessitates close supervision.

Chatbots and virtual agents serve as administrative officers, tax consultants, legal assistants, immigration advisors, and health triage bots.

They take care of mundane questions, freeing up human civil servants to work on more complicated projects.

3.4. AI in Public Administration: The Path to Zero Bureaucracy

By automating repetitive operations, simplifying procedures, and facilitating data-driven decision-making, Artificial Intelligence (AI) in public administration is revolutionizing conventional bureaucratic institutions. AI lowers human error, cuts down on delays, and gets rid of unnecessary processes through intelligent workflow management, predictive analytics, and digital service delivery.

This change brings governments closer to the goal of "*Zero Bureaucracy*," which would allow citizens to obtain services in a timely, effective, and transparent manner.

AI frees up human administrators from tedious work so they can concentrate on citizen involvement, policy review, and strategic planning. Strong governance structures, moral supervision, and protections to guarantee accountability, openness, and fair access to AI-enabled public services are necessary to realize this ambition.

3.4.1. Routine Task Automation

The use of AI and digital systems to carry out time-consuming, repetitive, and standardized administrative duties in public administration is known as routine task automation. Processing applications, keeping data, setting up services, and answering questions from regular citizens are a few examples. Automating these processes boosts productivity, lowers error rates, and frees up human employees to concentrate on difficult, decision-making activities.

Routine job automation is a crucial step toward a more responsive, transparent, and citizen-centric government by reducing bureaucratic delays and optimizing workflows.

AI automates:

- Verification of documents,
- Approval of invoices,
- Payroll administration,
- Procurement procedures,
- Court case triaging, and
- Updating of records.

This removes the possibility of corruption, delays, and human mistake.

3.4.2. Predictive Management

In public administration, predictive management is *the use of Artificial Intelligence (AI) and data analytics to foresee future trends, issues, and citizen requirements before they completely materialize.* AI can predict public service demand, spot possible bottlenecks, and optimize resource allocation by examining past data, current inputs, and behavioural trends. This proactive strategy lessens problems and inefficiencies by enabling governments to develop policies, assign staff, and distribute funds more effectively.

Predictive management improves responsiveness, efficacy, and public happiness by changing governance from reactive problem-solving to strategic, forward-looking decision-making. School enrolment requirements, hospital demand, water and power use, criminal areas, and food security issues are all predicted by AI.

Real-time optimisation takes the place of lengthy planning periods in predictive governance.

3.4.3. Transitioning from Reactive to Proactive Management

The *change in public administration made possible by AI is known as "Transitioning from Reactive to Proactive Management," in which governments predict problems and take action before they become more serious rather than reacting after the fact.*

Through the use of predictive analytics, real-time monitoring, and data-driven insights, authorities are able to recognize new issues, such as infrastructure requirements, public service demands, or societal trends, and promptly address them.

This proactive strategy represents a substantial shift from traditional, reaction-based government to an adaptive, forward-thinking, and intelligent public administration model by lowering inefficiencies, averting catastrophes, and raising citizen satisfaction.

AI anticipates issues rather than reacting to them:

- Preventing infrastructure breakdown;
- Redirecting traffic before traffic jams;
- Focussing on welfare before poverty worsens; and
- Deploying police before crime increases.

PATRICK MUKOSHA

Foresight replaces firefighting in government.

3.5. Digital Identity: The Basis for Intelligent Governance

A safe, unified, and verifiable electronic representation of a citizen's identification that facilitates easy communication with government systems is referred to as a "*Digital Identity.*" Digital identity is the cornerstone of intelligent government, enabling citizens to securely and effectively engage in digital civic processes, authenticate transactions, and access public services.

Digital identification, when combined with AI, improves transparency, lowers fraud, simplifies administration, and allows for personalised service delivery. In an increasingly data-driven state, strong cybersecurity measures, privacy protections, and legal safeguards are necessary to maintain confidence, stop abuse, and defend citizens' rights.

AI-powered public services are accessible through a secure digital identity system.

3.5.1. **Elements of Digital Identity:**

- Blockchain digital certificates;
- Electronic ID cards;
- Mobile ID apps;
- Biometric verification (facial recognition, fingerprints).

3.5.2. Advantages: Fraud protection, rapid authentication, safe transactions, and precise demographic analytics are all made possible by digital IDs.

1. **Dangers and Precautions**

- Identity theft;

- Privacy violations;
- Concerns about surveillance.

Strict data protection regulations, encryption guidelines, and open governance structures are necessary for this.

3.6. Digital Justice and AI Courts

The use of Artificial Intelligence into legal institutions to improve effectiveness, consistency, and access to justice is referred to as "digital justice" and "AI courts." AI can help courts by automating mundane legal processes, managing case backlogs, evaluating legal precedents, and supporting sentencing guidelines. Digital platforms make justice more accessible and transparent by facilitating electronic filing, remote hearings, and quicker dispute settlement.

Even if AI increases efficiency and consistency, human judges must still make ultimate decisions in order to maintain justice, moral reasoning, and due process. To avoid prejudice, defend rights, and preserve public confidence in AI-assisted judicial systems, robust legal frameworks are crucial.

Legal systems are infamous for their inefficiencies, backlogs, and delays. AI has the potential to revolutionise the administration of justice.

3.6.1. Case Management Driven by AI

AI organises situations according to their urgency, complexity, level of knowledge needed, and likelihood of a speedy resolution.

3.6.2. Online Courts

AI facilitates remote judgements, schedules hearings, and handles electronic evidence.

3.6.3. Smart Tools for Legal Research

AI helps courts and attorneys by summarising legal arguments, identifying errors, and analysing case precedents.

Justice becomes more accessible, equitable, and quicker.

3.7. Smart Cities: E-Government's Living Laboratories 2.0 Cities are evolving into digital beings.

The living labs of E-Government 2.0, where digital government is tested, improved, and experienced in real time, are represented by *Smart Cities*. Cities are becoming more and more like digital entities, constantly perceiving, learning, and reacting to their surroundings thanks to AI, IoT sensors, big data, and connected infrastructure.

These systems let governments to make quick, data-driven choices and provide responsive public services by monitoring traffic, energy use, public safety, health services, and environmental factors. Smart cities serve as living laboratories that show how digital governments may function in a dynamic and adaptable manner.

However, they also raise important issues around data governance, inclusion, democratic accountability, and surveillance in more sophisticated urban ecosystems.

3.7.1. Traffic Management using AI

AI keeps an eye on roadways and Traffic light adjustments, vehicle rerouting, peak congestion prediction, and accident reduction.

3.7.2. Intelligent Utilities

AI manages power and water systems, identifying leaks, forecasting shortages, and maximising energy distribution.

3.7.3. Emergency Response and Public Safety

By evaluating CCTV data, identifying suspicious trends, forecasting the effects of disasters, and streamlining emergency response routes, Artificial Intelligence improves safety.

Smart cities become more efficient, safer, and cleaner.

3.8. AI as an Integrity Engine in the Battle against Corruption

The term "AI as an integrity engine" describes *the application of AI to identify, stop, and discourage corruption in governmental processes.* AI can find irregularities, suspicious trends, and conflicts of interest that can point to corrupt activities by examining massive amounts of financial transactions, procurement records, public expenditure data, and administrative decisions. Automated monitoring promotes transparency in public administration, decreases human discretion, and restricts potential for manipulation.

As a result, AI promotes fair governance, increases trust in public institutions, and fosters accountability—as long as it is applied with strict monitoring, legal protections, and moral guidelines to avoid abuse or selective enforcement.

Transparency is strengthened by AI through:

3.8.1. Financial Audits That Are Automated

AI monitors financial transactions, identifies irregularities, and stops embezzlement.

3.8.2. Open Purchasing

Algorithms keep an eye on procurement to identify price inflation, collusion, conflicts of interest, and fraudulent suppliers.

3.8.3. Platforms for Protecting Whistle-blowers

AI protects anonymous reporting platforms and promotes integrity.

AI takes on the role of public trust protector.

3.9. Inclusive Governance – Leaving No Citizen Behind

In the digital era, *inclusive governance focusses on using AI and technology to guarantee that all citizens may access and profit from government services and decision-making processes, regardless of their location, income, gender, age, or ability*. Personalised service delivery, multilingual communication, assistive technologies, and focused social initiatives that cater to the needs of vulnerable and marginalised groups are all made possible by AI.

Inclusive governance enhances social cohesiveness and democratic involvement by lowering barriers, increasing accessibility, and encouraging fair policy outcomes.

However, closing the digital divide, guaranteeing equitable algorithmic design, and integrating equity and human rights at the heart of intelligent governance systems are all necessary to achieve real inclusion.

AI guarantees service access for under-represented populations.

1. **Interfaces for Assistance**

   Voice-based applications, sign language recognition, and disability accessibility solutions are all supported by AI.

1. **Access in Rural Areas**

   AI mobile units use satellite-based communication, mobile e-government vans, and drones to deliver services to remote places.

1. **Localisation of Language**

AI rapidly transforms public information into regional tongues.
Global governance is achieved.

3.10. E-Government Risks 2.0

The advanced and new issues that emerge when governments implement AI-driven, data-intensive, and highly interconnected digital governance systems are referred to as "e-government risks 2.0." Cybersecurity hazards, extensive data breaches, algorithmic bias, system malfunctions, and an excessive reliance on automated decision-making are some of these risks. Inadequate regulation of centralised data systems and increased digital surveillance may also jeopardise public trust, civil liberties, and privacy.

Furthermore, social exclusion may worsen due to unequal access to digital infrastructure. Strong cybersecurity frameworks, transparent algorithms, moral AI standards, legal protections, and ongoing human monitoring are all need to manage these dangers as e-government develops and guarantee that digital governance stays safe, just, and accountable.

3.10.1. **Online Dangers**

Hackers frequently attack government systems.

3.10.2. Bias in Algorithms

To guarantee equity in:

- Welfare distribution,
- Law enforcement, and
- The distribution of public resources, AI must be audited.

3.10.3. **Excessive Monitoring**

Smart systems run the possibility of being used as authoritarian control mechanisms.

3.10.4. **Exclusion from Digital**

People who are illiterate or lack gadgets could be excluded.

Adoption must be accompanied by robust policy frameworks and public education initiatives.

3.11. The Future: Completely Independent Governance?

The concept of fully autonomous governance envisions a time where AI systems manage public services, carry out policies, and make administrative decisions on their own with little assistance from humans. Although highly automated administration is now feasible because to technical advancements, totally autonomous AI-led government is still implausible and undesirable because of ethical, legal, and democratic issues. Value judgements, moral accountability, and social legitimacy are all components of governance that AI cannot have on its own.

Deeply enhanced governance, *in which humans maintain ultimate power, responsibility, and moral oversight while AI manages efficiency, prediction, and execution, is increasingly likely to occur in the future*. This equilibrium guarantees that governance continues to be both human-centered and intelligent.

Imagine a government in which:

- Taxes are self-calculating;
- Budgets are automatically adjusted;
- Welfare distribution is completely automated;
- Permits are given instantaneously;
- Decisions are data-driven; and
- Citizens engage with the government without any friction.

This is happening; it's not idealistic.

The next frontier in public administration is autonomous government.

In conclusion, the intelligent state is built on e-government 2.0. It increases national competitiveness, efficiency, accountability, transparency, trust, and convenience.

AI turns governance from a burden into an experience that citizens can engage with ease, speed, and assurance.

Future governments will be more than just digital.

It is very citizen-centered, astute, and proactive.

Chapter 4: The Power of Data: AI's Understanding of Society

Overview

Artificial Intelligence doesn't function in a vacuum; it consumes data, develops from patterns, and makes decisions based on the insights it gathers. This turns data in politics from a passive record of society into an active force that can influence public opinion, participation, and governance. AI-driven political systems rely heavily on data, and mastering contemporary leadership requires an understanding of how AI uses data to interpret society.

This chapter examines how data becomes intelligence, how information becomes political advantage, and how AI reads countries the way analysts used to read polls.

4.1. Data as Power: The New Political Resource

Information from surveys, reports, community input, newspapers, and intelligence briefings has long been used by political leaders. However, AI alters the scope and accuracy of what is feasible.

Important changes:

- AI examines behaviour, communication, and sentiment across millions of people, from sample sizes to complete population insights.
- From periodic data to real-time intelligence: *Leaders can instantaneously gauge public sentiment in place of quarterly surveys.*
- From descriptive to predictive power: *AI foresees impending social problems before they arise.*

Consequences for Governance:

- Leaders are better able to comprehend the concerns of the public.
- Policies can focus on actual needs rather than hypothetical ones.
- It is possible to optimise resource allocation with greater assurance.

Data has evolved from a support tool to a strategic political asset.

4.2. Data Sources in Contemporary Politics

Data is becoming more and more important in today's politics. Large streams of political data have been produced by the digitization of society, government, and civic participation. These data streams influence how choices are made, power is used, and public opinion is perceived. To guide strategy, policy creation, and political communication, contemporary political actors—governments, parties, campaigns, interest groups, and foreign policy institutions—now rely on a variety of data sources.

1. **Voter and Electoral Information**

The foundation of political data analysis consists of voter registration databases, electoral rolls, turnout records, and past voting trends. Political organizations can use these databases to track participation trends, identify voting blocs, and create focused mobilization plans. Election data allows for accurate voter segmentation when paired with demographic information like age, locality, and educational attainment.

1. **Census and Demographic Information**

Fundamental information about population size, distribution, income levels, employment, ethnicity, and education is provided by national censuses and demographic surveys. Such information is utilized in politics for long-term development planning, social policy formulation, resource allocation, and constituency delineation. Future political realignments are frequently indicated by changes in the population.

1. **Digital Footprint and Social Media Information**

Real-time data on popular mood, political debate, and issue salience is produced via platforms including Facebook, Instagram, YouTube, TikTok, and X (Twitter). Analysts can track opinion patterns, identify new narratives, and evaluate the efficacy of political communications through likes, shares, comments, hashtags, and network interactions. This information is essential to contemporary agenda-setting and advocacy.

1. **News and Media Information**

Both organized and unstructured information about political events, elite remarks, policy discussions, and framing can be found in traditional and digital news sources. In order to comprehend how issues are communicated to the public and how narratives change over time and space, media monitoring systems examine tone, frequency, and framing.

1. **Development and Economic Measures**

Political decision-making is directly impacted by data from central banks, financial ministries, international organizations, and statistical agencies, including employment statistics, debt levels, trade flows, inflation rates, and poverty indices. Election campaigns, public confidence in leadership performance, and budget priorities are all influenced by economic data.

1. **Administrative and Governance Information**

Records of public service delivery, procurement, taxation, and regulatory compliance are examples of government-generated data. Initiatives for institutional reform, performance monitoring, anti-corruption campaigns, and evidence-based policymaking are all supported by these databases.

1. **Geopolitical and Security Information**

In both national security and international policy, conflict databases, crime statistics, migration patterns, border activities, satellite images, and intelligence evaluations are essential. Such data is increasingly processed by AI systems to evaluate risk, forecast instability, and aid in military or diplomatic decision-making—all of which raise serious ethical and sovereignty issues.

1. **Data From Surveys, Polls, And Opinion Research**

Attitudes, opinions, and values are recorded through focus groups, public opinion polls, and long-term surveys. When combined with behavioural and digital data, these data sources continue to be essential for comprehending voter priorities, institutional trust, and policy approval.

1. **International Databases and Open Data**

Accessible datasets on governance, human rights, the climate, development, and political stability are available through open government portals and international organizations. These resources facilitate independent analysis, increase transparency, and facilitate cross-national comparisons.

1. New Sources of Information

Biometric systems, geolocation data, mobile phone information, and AI-generated prediction models are examples of new data streams that are starting to have an impact on politics. Despite their strength, they pose significant concerns around consent, privacy, monitoring, and democratic accountability.

Data is more than just information in modern politics; it is strategic power.

Institutions and leaders who are able to responsibly gather, analyse, and manage political data have a clear advantage. However, ethical data use, robust legal frameworks, and public confidence in the creation and use of political data are all necessary for democratic resilience.

The outcome is a leadership approach that is based on facts rather than gut feeling.

4.3. How AI Processes Political Data

AI uses a methodical pipeline to filter political data, turning unprocessed data into useful insights for strategy and decision-making. First, AI systems gather information from a variety of sources, including public records, surveys, social media activity, voter registration, census data, news media, and economic indicators. This material is frequently extensive, unorganised, and updated frequently.

AI then handles data integration and cleaning, combining datasets into a single analytical framework while eliminating mistakes, duplication, and inconsistencies. AI then examines trends in public opinion, political speech, voting behaviour, and demographics using machine learning and natural language processing (NLP). For instance, NLP analyses news stories, social media posts, and speeches to identify viewpoints, feelings, and developing narratives.

AI also *uses segmentation algorithms to divide voters into categories according to their interests, opinions, and propensity for support, and predictive analytics to predict election results, policy responses, turnout rates, or social unrest.* In order to help leaders and campaigns make data-driven decisions, customise communications, allocate resources effectively, and react quickly to political dynamics, the results are finally displayed through dashboards, simulations, and recommendations.

Diagram: How AI collects and Processes Political data

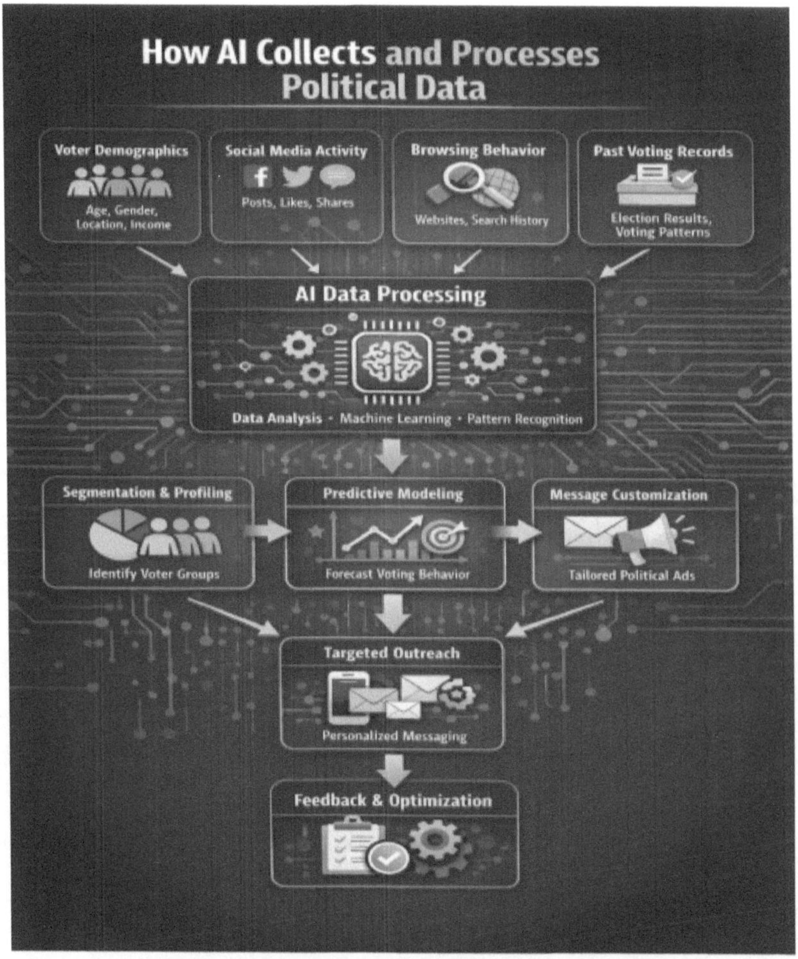

Figure 4: How AI Collects and Processes Political Data

***Figure 4**: Illustrates how AI collects, processes (Segmentation & Profiling, Message Customisation and Predictive modelling) and disseminates political data, including receiving feedback and system optimisation.*

In short, AI Data Processing Steps are as follows:

1. **Data Collection:** Information is collected from various streams and integrated into centralized systems;

2. **Cleaning**: AI eliminates duplicates, errors, noise, and irrelevant information—creating structured, trustworthy datasets;

3. **Pattern Detection**:

AI machine learning identifies:

- Voting behaviour trends;
- Demographic shifts;
- Political polarization zones;
- Social concerns gaining momentum;

4. **Prediction AI models forecast**:

- Upcoming political crises;
- Likely election outcomes;
- Successful or unsuccessful messaging strategies;
- Public engagement plans.

4.4. Political Psychology and Behavioural Insights

Understanding how emotions, beliefs, cognitive biases, and social influences determine political attitudes and decision-making is the main goal of political psychology and behavioural insights. *Governments and political players can better comprehend motivation, trust, fear, identity, and persuasion by using AI to analyse trends in voter behaviour, sentiment, and responses to political communications.*

The reasons behind citizens' support for particular leaders or programs, the ways in which narratives and framing shape public opinion, and the ways in which group dynamics impact political engagement are all explained by behavioural insights. Strong ethical bounds and transparency are essential since, when utilised improperly, these insights run the risk of manipulation and psychological exploitation.

However, when employed ethically, they facilitate more effective communication, policy creation, and public involvement.

Thus, this is the point at which AI becomes both analytical and psychological.

AI *learns why people act the way they do, not just what they do.*

AI is able to deduce emotional states, political grievances, ideological inclinations, levels of trust in leadership, and social group dynamics.

These insights provide leaders with an unparalleled comprehension of:

- *Which communications will mobilise?*
- *Which policies will resonate? and*
- *Which issues need immediate attention?*

This enhances governance in the hands of moral leaders.

It can be manipulative in the wrong hands.

4.5. Predictive Governance's Ascent

The growing use of AI and data analytics to predict social trends, citizen needs, and possible policy outcomes, allowing governments to act proactively rather than reactively, is known as "*Predictive Governance's Ascent*." AI systems can predict changes in the economy, public health issues, social unrest, and environmental effects by examining past data, current knowledge, and behavioural patterns.

Policymakers may *create focused responses, distribute resources effectively, and reduce risks before they worsen thanks to this predictive capacity*. Predictive governance improves efficiency, responsiveness, and evidence-based decision-making, but it also necessitates close supervision to avoid prejudice, an excessive dependence on algorithms, and the possible degradation of human judgement in democratic government.

The future of political administration is predictive governance, which is already beginning to take shape. Food shortages, unemployment spikes, predicted protest locations, industries in need of subsidies, possible political upsets, and policy acceptance trajectories are all things that AI can predict.

Predictive model-savvy governments may address national issues before they escalate into crises, fostering stability and public confidence.

4.6. Dangers: Monitoring, Prejudice, and Misunderstanding

AI poses serious risks as it gets more and more integrated into governance, such as intrusive monitoring, algorithmic bias, and systemic misinterpretation. *Monitoring* is the term used to describe widespread surveillance of persons' communications, behaviours, and actions, which can jeopardise civil liberties and privacy. When biased data or faulty algorithms result in discriminatory outcomes that perpetuate social injustices and marginalise disadvantaged populations, *prejudice results*.

When AI *misinterprets* intricate social, cultural, or political circumstances, it might result in incorrect policy recommendations or poorly informed decisions. To guarantee that AI serves the public good without jeopardising trust, justice, or democratic ideals, these threats highlight the necessity of ethical frameworks, human oversight, openness, and rigorous testing.

There are significant risks associated with great power.

Among the main risks are:

1. **Surveillance Overreach**: AI has the ability to monitor actions to the point where privacy may be violated.

2. **Bias in Data:** Biased data will lead to biased AI decisions, which will result in unfairness in public service hiring, welfare distribution, police, and political propaganda.

3. **Data Misinterpretation:** AI is able to identify relationships that people would miss. Leaders must be sufficiently knowledgeable about AI to confront it.

4. **AI's politicisation:** A ruling party's AI systems can be utilised against its adversaries.

4.7. Constructing Democratic, Ethical Data Systems

Designing AI and data infrastructures that support accountability, transparency, fairness, and citizen rights within governance is essential to building democratic, ethical data systems. In addition to preventing bias and discrimination, these systems guarantee that data collection, storage, and analysis respect privacy, consent, and inclusion. They include systems that allow for citizen supervision, decision explanation, and algorithm auditing.

Democratic, moral data systems enable governments to make evidence-based decisions while upholding social justice, preserving public confidence, and defending fundamental rights. In the digital age, these frameworks are crucial for striking a balance between the potential of AI and the values of justice, accountability, and democratic government.

Leaders must create systems that are:

- Transparent;
- Accountable;
- Privacy-respecting;
- Inclusive of all demographics; and
- Independent from partisan influence if they want AI in politics to help democracy rather than damage it.

Important design principles, oversight organisations, data governance regulations, algorithmic audits, public feedback loops, and fairness requirements.

AI that is responsible makes sure that the people, not the political elite, benefit from the technology.

4.8. Final Thoughts: Information as the New Political Guide

Information is now essential to strategy, governance, and citizen engagement in today's political environment. This change is accelerated by AI, which turns enormous amounts of data into useful insights that allow for evidence-based decision-making, targeted communications, and predictive policy. With previously unheard-of accuracy, leaders can now foresee the requirements of the public, proactively address new problems, and allocate resources as efficiently as possible.

However, in order to avoid manipulation, bias, and the deterioration of democratic values, the power of information must be balanced with ethical responsibility, transparency, and human judgement. In the end, information is more than just a tool in the age of intelligent government; it is the compass that directs political activity and advances society.

Political leadership has changed as a result of AI's capacity to comprehend society via data.

Leaders that adopt data-driven governance will:

- Create more intelligent policies;
- Communicate more successfully;
- Identify problems early; and
- Establish trust by accuracy.

In a world where data is the new compass for nations, those who oppose this change will lag behind.

Those who can sense society's digital pulse and use it for the benefit of society as a whole will have the political future.

Chapter 5: AI and Elections: The New Democratic Machine

Overview

Elections are the pulse of democracy. They choose leaders, set the course of the country, and give governance legitimacy. *Elections in the past mostly relied on human-centered procedures, such as ballot paper systems, physical campaigning, opinion polls, and manual registration*. But *today, elections are becoming data-driven, predictive, and hyper-targeted due to artificial intelligence*.

AI is now an unseen but potent force that is changing how elections are conducted, how voters are perceived, how ballots are safeguarded, and how outcomes are predicted. This chapter examines how Artificial Intelligence is transforming 21st-century democracy and electoral politics.

5.1. The Election Campaign Driven by AI

Artificial Intelligence is used in AI-driven election campaigns to change the way political candidates interact with people, craft narratives, and maximise resources. AI finds important voter groups, forecasts turnout, and crafts messages that appeal to certain audiences by examining enormous databases, such as voter demographics, social media activity, historical voting behaviour, and public mood. While machine learning models continuously test and improve messaging for optimum impact, automated systems oversee email campaigns, social media posts, and digital ads.

Rapid scenario simulations made possible by AI enable campaigns to predict opponent tactics and audience responses. This strategy raises ethical questions about transparency, privacy, and manipulation while improving efficiency, accuracy, and response, radically changing contemporary political campaigning.

These days, political campaigns are designed with algorithms rather than just slogans.

Important changes made possible by AI include:

- Predictive voter modelling in place of guesswork;
- Micro-targeted communications in place of generic speeches;
- AI-driven strategy simulations in place of intuition; real-time mood monitoring in place of static polling.

AI-powered campaigns become faster and more precise, increasing their effectiveness and impact.

5.2. Analysis of Predictive Voter Behaviour

Based on past trends, demographic data, social media activity, and behavioural indicators, predictive voter behaviour analysis employs Artificial Intelligence (AI) and data analytics to predict how people or groups are likely to vote. In order to model voter proclivities, machine learning algorithms find correlations between variables including age, geography, income, education, online involvement, and issue preferences. Campaigns can use predictive analysis to segment groups, predict voter turnout, and create tailored message that maximises mobilisation and persuasion.

Although this method improves strategic accuracy, it also raises moral questions regarding privacy, manipulation, and the possible reinforcing of prejudices, underscoring the necessity of using predictive insights in political processes in a responsible and open manner.

Political strategists can use AI to forecast voters' opinions both now and in the future.

How Voter Behaviour Is Analysed By AI

- Votes can be grouped according to their interests, fears, and aspirations;
- Voter participation can be predicted;
- Swing votes who are indecisive can be accurately identified; and
- Ideological changes over time can be mapped.

Campaign teams now have an unparalleled capacity to modify strategy and message with mathematical assurance.

5.3. Micro-targeting: Tailored Political Communications

One of the most revolutionary and contentious use of AI in elections is micro-targeting.

Micro-Targeting: What is it?

The use of AI and data analytics to send highly customised political messaging to certain people or voter segments is known as micro-targeting. Campaigns can create messages that speak to an individual's particular interests, values, and concerns by examining demographics, internet behaviour, social media activity, and historical voting trends. Compared to broad, generalised messages, this enables political players to more successfully sway opinions, boost engagement, and inspire voter action. Micro-targeting raises ethical concerns about privacy, manipulation, transparency, and the potential to exacerbate social and political polarisation, even while it improves campaign precision and efficiency.

Diagram: Micro-Targeting: Tailored Political Communications

Figure 5: Micro-Targeting: Tailored Political Communications

AI IN POLITICS: THE RISE OF ALGORITHMIC GOVERNANCE

***Figure** 5: Shows how AI micro-targets tailored political communications (targeted political messages) to the public.*

Delivering highly tailored political messages to particular groups, or even individuals, depending on their data profile is the technique.

First-time young voters, retirees worried about pensions, farmers impacted by climate change, urban professionals focused on taxes, and unemployed groups looking for job creation programs are a few examples of micro-targeted groups.

Benefits include improved voter engagement, more pertinent message, and increased mobilization and conversion.

Dangers: The establishment of "information silos," manipulation by emotive targeting, and covert political influence. Elections in the US, UK, Kenya, India, and Brazil have already been altered by micro-targeting, and its influence will only increase.

5.4. AI-Powered Content Development for Campaigns

The term "AI-powered content development" describes *the creation, management, and optimisation of political campaign materials using Artificial Intelligence on various platforms.* AI can produce speeches, social media postings, emails, ads, and visual media that are suited to certain audiences by utilising natural language processing, machine learning, and data analytics. It can find the best narratives, test and improve messaging in real time, and keep campaign branding constant. Campaigns may scale their communication operations, react quickly to events, and consistently engage voters with this strategy. However, there are moral questions concerning authenticity, false information, and the possibility of influencing public opinion when AI is used to create content.

Speeches, social media posts, campaign slogans, video scripts, targeted emails, and policy summaries are all now written by AI algorithms.

What used to require a group of strategists can now be completed in a matter of minutes.

Benefits

- Consistent messaging;
- Quick flexibility;
- A/B testing of political language; and
- The capacity to react quickly to emerging events.

Strategic Impact

AI-enhanced parties have a significant edge because campaigns can run continuously without taxing human personnel.

5.5. Using AI to Fight False Information

AI is being used more and more to identify, stop, and refute misinformation in public and political discourse. AI systems are able to detect false information, misinformation, and deepfakes in social media, news sites, and online interactions by using machine learning, natural language processing, and pattern recognition. These algorithms track the propagation of misleading narratives, flag dubious information, confirm facts, and even produce corrective messages to educate the public.

AI helps preserve information integrity, safeguard democratic processes, and lessen the impact of fake news on society by facilitating quick detection and response. In order to maintain AI interventions' transparency, objectivity, and accountability while upholding the right to free speech, ethical deployment is essential.

Although AI has the potential to propagate false information, it is also the most powerful weapon against it.

By identifying bot-driven campaigns, detecting deepfakes and fake news, flagging altered videos, tracking questionable online behaviour, and monitoring hostile foreign influence, Artificial Intelligence safeguards elections.

Democracies that are successful invest in AI not just to win

Successful democracies use AI to safeguard election integrity as well as to win elections.

5.6. AI in Election Administration and Voter Registration

By increasing accuracy, efficiency, and security throughout the electoral process, Artificial Intelligence (AI) improves election administration and voter registration. In **Voter Registration**, AI systems can verify identities, detect duplicates, update records, and ensure compliance with legal requirements. **During Elections**, AI helps manage polling logistics, predict turnout, allocate resources, and monitor for irregularities or fraudulent activity. By analysing data in real time, AI can optimise the voting process, reduce errors, and enhance transparency.

While AI increases operational efficiency, protect citizen data, and preserve public confidence in democratic institutions. AI is being used by governments all around the world to update their election systems.

Applications for managing elections:

- Automated voter registration checks;
- Fraudulent ID detection;
- Duplicate voter detection;
- Intelligent biometric verification;
- Strategically placed voting places; and
- Predictive resource allocation.

Positives

- Decreases fraud;
- Lowers administrative expenses;
- Guarantees quicker, more seamless voting procedures; and
- Increases public confidence in the outcome.

AI IN POLITICS: THE RISE OF ALGORITHMIC GOVERNANCE

Elections are becoming precision-engineered rather than manual thanks to AI.

5.7. AI and Election Cybersecurity: Protecting the Digital Vote

The deliberate use of AI and data analytics to target particular voter segments with highly customised political messages is known as *Micro-Targeting*. Campaigns can create communications that closely connect with people's interests, values, and concerns by examining voter demographics, prior behaviour, social media activity, and issue preferences. By using customised communications instead of general, generic appeals, this strategy improves voter mobilisation, engagement, and persuasion.

Despite its effectiveness, micro-targeting highlights the need for transparency and responsible use of voter data by posing ethical questions about privacy, manipulation, and the potential to exacerbate political polarisation.

Digital threats are the new political battlefield.

AI is essential for protecting electoral systems from:

- Hacking;
- Denial-of-service Attacks;
- Data breaches;
- Ransomware;
- Foreign influence, and
- Insider manipulation.

Anomaly detection algorithms and automated intrusion prevention systems are important AI security tools.

Voting audits supported by blockchain technology; real-time threat intelligence

AI is the barrier that keeps democracy from collapsing in the event of a single hack.

5.8. Predicting Election Results: From Survey to Forecast

From the days of straightforward opinion polls to extremely complex forecasting models that incorporate statistical analysis, behavioural research, and AI-driven simulations, election prediction has undergone significant change. In the past, surveys and sampling techniques were largely used to forecast elections. Voters in random or stratified samples were asked who they planned to support, and the findings were then extrapolated to reflect the entire community.

These techniques were helpful, but they frequently had drawbacks, such as sample bias, nonresponse bias, and the difficulty of identifying late fluctuations in voter sentiment.

In order to increase accuracy, election forecasting now incorporates several data layers. Predictive models include the following in addition to conventional surveys:

- **Historical Voting Patterns:** They examine past election outcomes to find patterns in voter behaviour.
- **Socioeconomic And Demographic Data:** assessing how variables like geography, age, income, and education affect voting patterns.
- **Sentiment Analysis and Real-Time Polling:** These use digital interaction, social media, and search patterns to record shifting public opinion.
- **Economic Indicators and Issue Salience:** taking into account how factors like inflation, unemployment, or healthcare issues affect voter choices.

AI-driven forecasting systems and political analysts employ sophisticated algorithms that simulate various election scenarios and give probabilities to results instead of making deterministic forecasts.

Analysts are able to spot patterns, possible shocks, and crucial combat regions since these forecasts are dynamic and constantly change as new information becomes available.

For instance, forecasters can estimate results at fine-grained spatial levels while accounting for demographic aspects by using methods such as *Multilevel Regression with Post-Stratification* (MRP). In a similar vein, ensemble forecasting—which integrates the results of several models—has been shown to be more dependable than depending solely on one survey or prediction technique.

In the end, forecasting election outcomes is now more about measuring uncertainty and probability than it is about speculating about who will win. Modern political forecasting offers a complex, data-driven view of the electoral landscape by combining surveys, historical data, and AI analytics, enabling parties, candidates, and the general public to make well-informed strategic decisions.

Diagram: Predicting Election Results - From Survey to Forecast

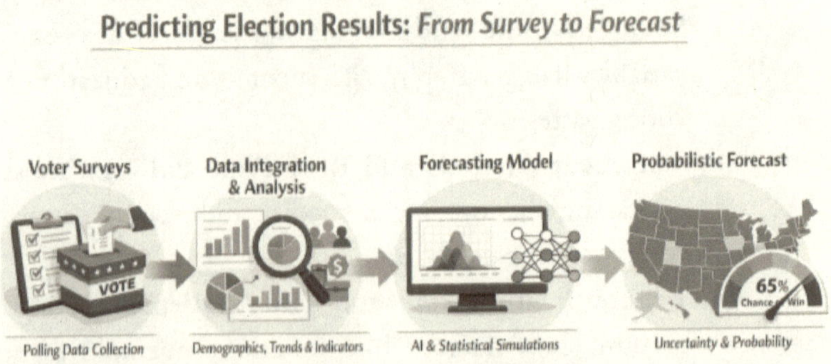

Figure 6: Predicting Election Result: From Survey to Forecast

Figure 6*: The diagram depicts how election results are predicted, from conducting surveys, data integration & analysis, to forecasting.*

Conventional polling is losing its relevance.

These days, election forecasting uses:

- Sentiment analysis;
- Ai election predicting;
- Economic statistics;
- Historical data;
- Demographic models;
- Real-time online discussions;
- Trends in migration and mobility.

Result

AI provides forecasts with levels of precision that were unthinkable ten years ago.

Thousands of scenarios can be simulated by campaign teams, such as:

- *"What if turnout increases by 10% in rural areas?"*
- *"What if young voters are more likely to support the opposition?"*
- *"What happens if urban support for the ruling party declines?"*

This enables strategists to prepare reactions in advance of events.

5.9. Legal and Ethical Issues with AI-Powered Elections

Artificial intelligence's incorporation into electoral procedures offers tremendous potential for accuracy, efficiency, and voter participation, but it also presents difficult moral and legal issues. Policymakers, technologists, and citizens must deal with issues that could jeopardise justice, transparency, and democratic integrity as AI becomes more prevalent in political campaigns, voter targeting, election administration, and even result prediction.

Legal Aspects

1. **Data Security and Privacy**: Large volumes of voter data, including as demographics, social media activity, and behavioural patterns, are essential to AI systems. This data must be collected, stored, and processed in accordance with privacy laws and regulations, such as national data protection acts or the General Data Protection Regulation (GDPR) in Europe. Legal liability and a decline in public confidence could result from unauthorised usage or violations.
2. **Election Law Compliance:** Campaign advertising, transparency, and political message are subject to stringent regulations in many countries. If messaging is not adequately controlled, AI-driven micro-targeting and automated content creation may unintentionally break these regulations, running the risk of penalties or legal action.
3. **Algorithmic Accountability:** Legal frameworks must specify accountability when AI systems have an impact on polls, vote counting, or campaign decision-making. Election legitimacy challenges may arise if an algorithm

displays bias or misreports results. Laws requiring audits, openness, and verifiability of AI systems used in elections may be necessary.

Ethical Considerations

1. **Bias and Discrimination**: The data used to train AI models is reflected in them. AI may disproportionately favour or disfavour particular voter groups, undercutting the idea of fair representation, if historical or societal biases are ingrained in these databases.
2. **Transparency and Explainability**: Algorithmic judgements, such voter targeting or content prioritisation, must be explicable in order for ethical AI to be used in elections. Voters and authorities ought to comprehend the rationale for the display of particular messages or the increased emphasis on particular campaign locations.
3. **Manipulation and Influence:** AI-driven tactics can be used to disseminate false information, manipulate voter mood, or take advantage of psychological weaknesses. The difference between coercive or misleading influence and persuasive advocacy must be addressed in ethical frameworks.
4. **Autonomy and Informed Consent:** Voters must be allowed to make their own decisions. When AI systems gently influence behaviour, possibly avoiding conscious decision-making, or when voters are not aware of how much AI affects their election environment, ethical issues can develop.

The Way Ahead

Legal and ethical frameworks must advance with AI technology in order to protect democratic processes. This entails:

- Putting in place thorough algorithmic audits to find bias and mistakes.
- Requiring open reporting on the use of AI in election administration and campaigns.
- Strengthening consent and data protection procedures.
- Creating impartial oversight organisations to keep an eye on AI's impact on elections.

Maintaining faith in election systems requires striking a balance between the power of AI and ethical standards and legal protections. While AI promises efficiency and insight, it may unintentionally undermine democratic justice if it is not carefully regulated.

Diagram: AI in Elections – Ethical & Legal Issues

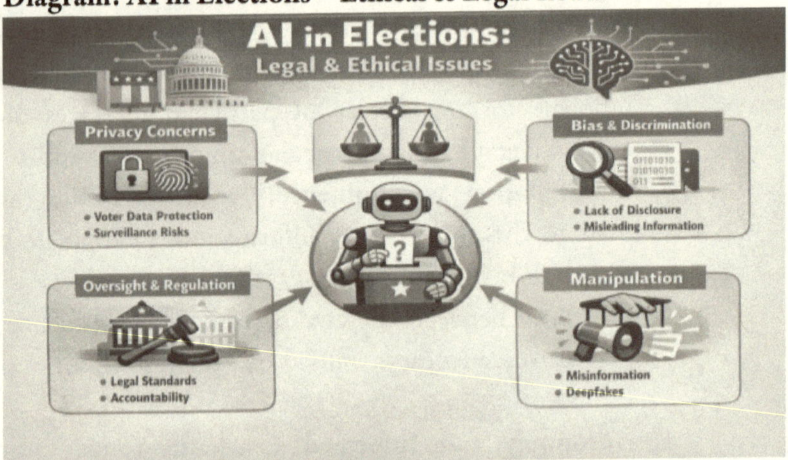

Figure 7: AI in Elections – Ethical & Legal Issues

***Figure** 7: Shows Legal and Ethical issues to be considered in an AI – powered Election system.*

Election-related AI poses previously unheard-of concerns. Important issues include:

1. **Violation of Privacy** - collecting voter information without permission.

2. **Manipulation** Emotion-based targeting that is unethical.

3. **Deepfake Propaganda** - AI-generated fake videos of candidates.

4. **International Influence** - foreign nations using AI systems as weapons.

5. **Bias in Algorithms** - favouring particular parties, ideas, or demographics.

Election laws must be updated by democracies to keep up with the power of AI.

5.10. Looking Ahead: AI-Powered Democratic Engagement

AI's influence on democratic participation is set to grow in previously unheard-of ways as the twenty-first century progresses. AI has the ability to change how people engage with public discourse, government, and policy-making in ways that go beyond simply improving campaigns or forecasting voter behaviour.

Increased civic engagement is one of the most promising options. AI-powered platforms can give citizens individualised information based on their communities and interests by giving them real-time access to policy debates, local government decisions, and legislative initiatives. These methods enable policymakers to better address the demands of constituents by identifying the topics that are most important to various demographic groups through the analysis of public opinion.

AI may also be advantageous for deliberative democracies, in which well-informed debate informs decision-making. Large-scale public discussion can be synthesised using sentiment analysis and natural language processing (NLP) to produce structured summaries that represent the range of opinions. By guaranteeing that all voices are heard without being muffled by the loudest participants, this might greatly increase the effectiveness of town halls, online consultations, and civic forums.

However, there are significant operational and ethical issues with the same authority. To avoid manipulation, false information, or the perpetuation of social biases, algorithms must be auditable and transparent. Furthermore, fair access is crucial; without it, AI-enhanced democracy runs the risk of widening already-existing digital gaps by favouring communities with better infrastructure and technology literacy.

AI IN POLITICS: THE RISE OF ALGORITHMIC GOVERNANCE

In the future, AI integration with democratic engagement is probably going to concentrate on three main areas:

1. **Predictive Policy Feedback:** Before laws are passed, citizens can anticipate possible outcomes by using AI to model the societal impact of proposed legislation.
2. **Adaptive Civic Platforms**: In order to promote more meaningful participation, these tools modify information and engagement prompts according to a citizen's knowledge, preferences, and previous interactions.
3. **Ethical Oversight Mechanisms**: Creating autonomous frameworks to guarantee that AI tools in democracies are responsible, equitable, and in line with the general welfare.

In the end, the promise of AI-powered democratic engagement is to enhance human judgement rather than to replace it. AI can contribute to the development of a more responsive society by giving individuals and policy-makers access to better information, deeper insights, and more channels of communication.

Diagram: AI-Powered Democratic Engagement

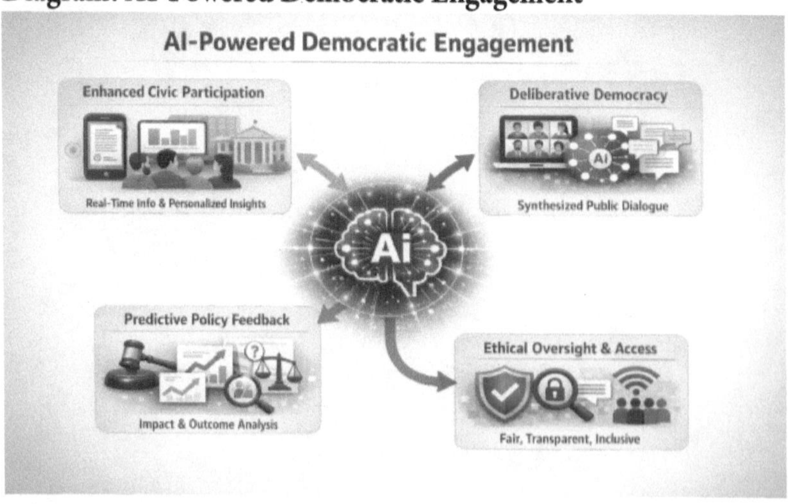

Figure 8: AI-Powered Democratic Engagement

Figure 8: *Shows how an AI-Powered Democratic Engagement enhances civic participation, enables deliberative democracy, ethical oversight & access and predictive policy feedback.*

Beyond elections, AI will redefine democratic participation.

AI-assisted policy voting, AI-moderated digital public forums, citizen-government interaction platforms, ballot information personalization voting systems, and AI-driven public education on political matters are some of the developing futures.

Democracy is changing from a sporadic activity (voting every few years) to an ongoing digital dialogue between citizens and leaders.

In conclusion: Elections in the Algorithmic Era

AI is now the new electoral apparatus. It affects how politicians run for office, how voters think, how ballots are secured, how outcomes are forecasted, and how democracy is formed. Adopting AI-driven voting systems will benefit countries with more responsive leadership, better-informed voters, and robust democratic processes. Those who oppose it will succumb to false information, ineffectiveness, and antiquated techniques.

To succeed in the upcoming political arena, politicians must comprehend Artificial Intelligence (AI), which will serve as the future referee, architect, and defender of democratic elections.

Chapter 6: Algorithmic Governance: Smarter States, Quicker Decisions

Overview

Governance has always developed in tandem with technological advancements.

Public knowledge was increased via the *Printing Press*.

The *Radio* brought nations together.

Communication became more accessible because to the *Internet*.

Artificial Intelligence is now the foundation of statecraft, allowing governments to rule with unmatched accuracy, speed, and vision.

Governance is changing dramatically in the digital age. Algorithmic systems are progressively supplementing and perhaps replacing traditional governmental mechanisms, which have historically relied on bureaucratic procedures, hierarchical decision-making, and sporadic human oversight. A world where nations can make quicker, data-driven, and more effective decisions is promised by this move towards algorithmic governance. However, efficiency entails complexity, and speed has political and ethical hazards.

A new leadership paradigm that is data-driven, predictive, and flexible is presented by the Algorithmic Age. This chapter looks at how AI is changing public service delivery, upgrading bureaucracy, changing governance structures, and redefining what constitutes an "effective state."

6.1. Algorithmic Governance Definition

Algorithmic governance is fundamentally about incorporating machine learning, artificial intelligence, and predictive analytics into public decision-making. To provide policymakers with useful insights, these systems examine enormous datasets, ranging from social media activity and economic indicators to satellite imagery and sensor networks. These days, governments can:

- Real-time detection of new economic or social trends.
- Automating standard administrative procedures, such resource distribution or tax collecting.
- Being prepared for emergencies, such as civil unrest, environmental catastrophes, or public health outbreaks.

Diagram: Algorithmic Governance – Smarter States, Quicker Decisions

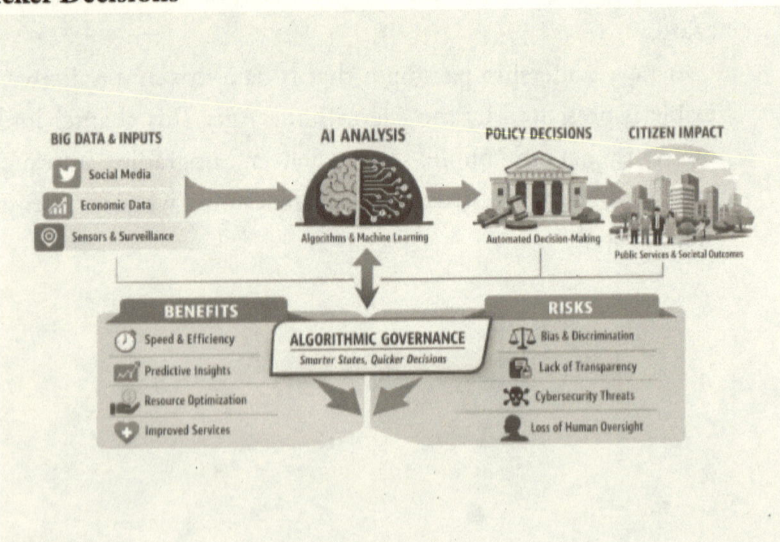

Figure 9: Algorithmic Governance – Smarter States, Quicker Decisions

Figure 9*: Illustrates how AI uses big data to analyse information for policy decisions and citizens engagement.*

Algorithmic governance is about predictive capacity, not just efficiency. Governments may now predict occurrences and take proactive measures instead of just responding to them.

6.2. Benefits of Algorithmic Governance

The application of AI and data-driven technologies to assist or automate government decision-making is known as algorithmic governance. When correctly planned and managed, it provides a number of significant advantages:

1. **Quicker and More Effective Decision-Making**

   Large volumes of data may be processed by algorithms in a matter of seconds, allowing governments to take swift action. For instance, AI systems can reduce traffic without waiting for human intervention by instantaneously analysing traffic patterns and modifying traffic lights in smart cities.

2. **Evidence-Based And Data-Driven Policies**

   Algorithmic governance depends on real-time data, in contrast to intuition-driven politics. Predictive analytics, for example, can assist health ministries in anticipating disease outbreaks and distributing vaccines or medical supplies before a crisis worsens.

3. **Decreased Corruption and Human Bias**

   Rules are consistently applied by automated systems. By spotting irregularities that people might miss or purposefully ignore, Artificial Intelligence (AI) might reduce favouritism and corruption in public procurement by flagging abnormal bidding patterns.

4. **Resource Optimisation and Cost Reduction**

By using AI to optimise resource allocation, governments may save money. AI-powered welfare systems, for instance, can identify fraudulent or duplicate claims, guaranteeing that the few available funds are distributed to those who are actually eligible.

5. **Better Public Service Provision**

Digital assistants and chatbots offer government services around-the-clock. Online applications for permits, tax status checks, and license renewals allow citizens to avoid lengthy lines and bureaucratic delays.

6. **Early Warning Systems and Predictive Governance**

Governments can foresee issues before they arise thanks to AI. Predictive models, for instance, can pinpoint areas that are at risk. Predictive models, for instance, can indicate areas vulnerable to flooding or food shortages, enabling early intervention and catastrophe planning.

7. **Increased Accountability and Transparency**

Decisions can be tracked and examined when algorithms are auditable. For instance, algorithmic scoring systems in social programs might increase public trust by demonstrating why a household was eligible for help or was not.

Algorithmic governance essentially turns the state from a reactive organisation into a proactive, intelligent system that can manage quickly, precisely, and foresightly while allowing human leaders to concentrate on strategy, morality, and accountability.

6.3. Algorithmic Governance's Practical Uses

Algorithmic governance is already influencing how contemporary nations function in a number of crucial areas; it is no longer only theoretical:

1. **Public Service Delivery:** AI-driven platforms are used by governments to automate ordinary services in public service delivery. For instance, citizens can access social welfare, healthcare, and tax services online thanks to digital ID systems connected to algorithms, which cut down on red tape, delays, and human gatekeeping.

2. **Public Safety and Law Enforcement:** Predictive analytics is used in public safety and law enforcement to better deploy patrols by analysing crime statistics. In order to prevent crime rather than just respond to it, cities employ algorithmic tools to detect crime hotspots based on historical patterns, time of day, and social variables.

3. **Healthcare Governance:** AI models are used in healthcare governance to forecast hospital demand and disease outbreaks by analysing population health data. Algorithms have been used to monitor infection patterns, control hospital capacity, and distribute vaccines according to risk profiles during pandemics.

4. **Economic And Financial Regulation:** Algorithmic systems are used in economic and financial regulation to track financial transactions in real time and identify instances of fraud, money laundering, and tax evasion. AI

is used by revenue authorities to identify questionable tax returns, increasing compliance and lowering the need for invasive audits.

5. **Urban Management and Smart Cities:** Algorithms regulate electricity grids, waste collection schedules, and transportation systems in urban management and smart cities. For instance, AI-powered energy systems balance the supply and demand of electricity to avoid blackouts, and smart traffic signals automatically adapt according to traffic levels.

6. **Social Policy and Welfare Administration**: Governments use algorithms in social policy and welfare administration to decide who is eligible for social assistance. These methods make sure that the most disadvantaged populations receive targeted help more effectively by evaluating data on employment, household size, and income.

7. **Environmental and Climate Governance**: AI uses satellite and sensor data to monitor pollution, deforestation, and climate threats in environmental and climate governance. Governments are able to detect illicit mining, monitor pollution, and send out early alerts for droughts or floods.

8. **Election Administration:** Algorithms are used in election administration to help with logistics planning, duplicate record detection, and voter registration management. AI tools reduce errors and disagreements by assisting election commissions in distributing voting materials in a fair and effective manner.

When taken as a whole, these applications show how algorithmic governance is turning the state into a digitally intelligent actor that can manage complexity at scale and change how public trust, power, and policy are used in the twenty-first century.

6.4. Algorithmic Governance's Challenges and Risks

Algorithmic governance is efficient and precise, but it also poses significant hazards that, if unchecked, might threaten democracy, justice, and public confidence.

Algorithmic bias and discrimination are a significant risk. Algorithms pick up knowledge from historical data, which frequently represents disparities from the past. Predictive police algorithms that are based on skewed crime statistics, for instance, could disproportionately target underprivileged or marginalised populations, perpetuating rather than resolving social inequities.

Lack of explainability and transparency is another major issue. Many AI systems function as "black boxes," making it challenging for citizens or even government authorities to comprehend the decision-making process. Accountability is compromised and confidence is undermined when an algorithm rejects citizen welfare payments or labels them as a security risk without providing a clear explanation.

Another major risk is *relying too much on automated decision-making*. Governments may give algorithms excessive power by viewing them as impartial and perfect. For example, when human judgement and compassion are ignored, mindlessly adhering to AI-generated risk rankings in criminal justice or immigration proceedings may result in unfair conclusions.

Data privacy and surveillance concerns provide additional hazard. Massive data collection, frequently comprising personal, biometric, or behavioural data, is essential to algorithmic governance. This can lead to invasive surveillance states where people are continuously observed, monitored, and profiled in the absence of robust safeguards.

Additionally, there is a chance of *inequity and digital isolation.* Citizens may be denied access to vital services if they lack digital tools, reliable internet, or digital literacy. For instance, rural communities, the elderly, and the impoverished may be disadvantaged by completely automated e-government systems.

Algorithmic governance is made more difficult by *cybersecurity risks and system manipulation.* AI systems are susceptible to manipulation, hacking, and fake data feeding. A hacked algorithm controlling energy grids, tax systems, or elections might create widespread upheaval.

Lastly, one of the biggest threats is *authoritarian abuse and political exploitation.* Algorithms can be used as a weapon to selectively enforce laws, stifle opposition, or rig elections. AI-driven governance may strengthen power rather than advance the common good in authoritarian environments.

Essentially, algorithmic governance has the potential to either subtly undermine or strengthen democratic institutions. The algorithmic state runs the potential of becoming efficient but unjust, unaccountable, and dangerously strong in the absence of transparency, ethical monitoring, legal protections, and human control.

6.5. Algorithmic Governance's Ethical and Political Repercussions

Power, accountability, and moral responsibility are all significantly altered by algorithmic governance in the political system. Its effects go well beyond technology; they are fundamental to ethics and democracy.

Algorithmic governance restructures authority and power in politics. *Technical systems created by engineers, data scientists, and private technology companies are increasingly making decisions instead of elected authorities and public employees.* For instance, political authority quietly shifts from parliaments to code—often created outside of democratic oversight—when an algorithm decides security risk scores or welfare eligibility.

The weakening of accountability is a significant ethical effect. *It's difficult to determine who is at fault when an algorithm makes a bad choice—the machine, the government agency, or the programmer?* Because voters are unable to readily contest or appeal computerised choices, this "responsibility gap" undermines democratic ideals.

Concerns of democratic legitimacy and consent are also raised by algorithmic governance. Leaders are chosen by the people, not by algorithms. Public engagement and discussion may decrease when regulations are successfully implemented by automated technologies, transforming governance into a technocratic process divorced from popular will.

Ethical bias disguising itself as neutrality is another effect. Despite the fact that algorithms incorporate human beliefs, presumptions, and political decisions, they are frequently seen as objective. For example, moral judgements about poverty, production, and worthiness—judgments concealed behind mathematical formulas—are reflected in a social scoring system that determines who gets aid.

Additionally, there is a chance that social control and widespread surveillance may become commonplace. AI-powered monitoring systems have the potential to redefine what constitutes appropriate state oversight. Without open political discussion, citizens may eventually come to accept continuous data collecting as the norm, undermining civil liberties and privacy.

Diagram: Algorithmic Governance's – Ethical and Political Repercussions

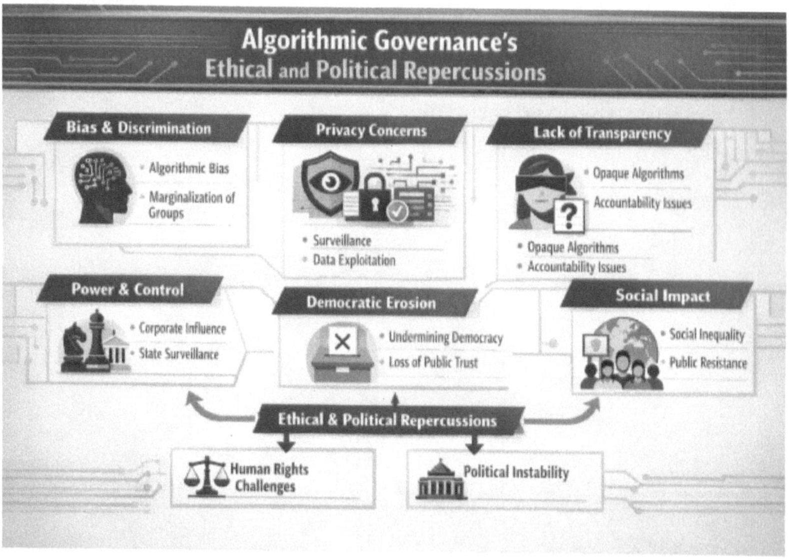

Figure 10: Algorithmic Governance's – Ethical and Political Repercussions

***Figure 10:** Illustrates how power, accountability, and moral responsibility are all significantly altered by algorithmic governance in the political system.*

If algorithmic governance is implemented without protections, it may reinforce authoritarian tendencies in politics. By effectively and covertly suppressing resistance, automated censorship, facial recognition, and predictive dissent monitoring can increase control while decreasing the overt use of force.

It is extremely problematic from an ethical standpoint to exclude human judgement, empathy, and moral reasoning. Algorithms are incapable of comprehending compassion, context, or extraordinary situations. An automated immigration or punishment system, for instance, can impose strict regulations while disregarding the humanitarian factors that characterise ethical government.

In conclusion, algorithmic governance compels society to address a crucial issue: should efficiency take precedence above moral responsibility and democratic discourse? Algorithmic governance runs the potential of producing a strong but morally bankrupt state that is effective in operation but brittle in legitimacy and trust if it lacks ethical frameworks, transparency, and human-in-the-loop scrutiny.

6.6. Transitioning to Smarter States

In order to create smarter governments, algorithmic governance must be included in a way that increases state capability without compromising human authority, democracy, or ethics. The objective is to create AI-augmented nations that govern more ethically, transparently, and intelligently rather than to replace government with robots.

Human-In-The-Loop governance is the first step towards a smarter state. Judges, public servants, and political leaders should be supported by algorithms rather than replaced by them. For instance, an AI system might suggest policy solutions based on data simulations, but responsible human authorities who are able to consider social, cultural, and moral aspects must still make the final judgements.

AI systems that are transparent and comprehensible are crucial. People need to be able to comprehend how decisions that impact their life are made. For example, the system should provide an appeals process and a clear explanation of the rationale utilised if an algorithm rejects a social benefit. AI becomes a tool of trust instead of a tool of control when it is transparent.

Strong ethical and legal foundations are also necessary for smarter nations. Where algorithms can be employed, what data they can access, and how their choices are reviewed must all be clearly defined by legislation. AI ethics commissions and legislative technology committees are examples of independent oversight organisations that support democratic control over automated systems.

Another aspect is *privacy protection and data governance.* A more intelligent state views citizen data as a public trust rather than a resource to be exploited. Strict permission regulations, anonymisation, and secure data infrastructures keep algorithmic control from merging with surveillance governance.

Building *government capacity* is equally important. In order for legislators, public officials, and courts to question, understand, and contest algorithmic outputs, states must invest in their digital literacy. Governments run the risk of being governed by systems they do not completely comprehend if they lack this understanding.

Inclusive digital transformation is a top priority for smarter states. All residents, especially those living in rural areas, the elderly, and those who are marginalised by technology, must benefit from AI-powered governance. Hybrid systems guarantee that no one is denied access to public services by fusing digital platforms with human service channels.

Lastly, *International Standards and Collaboration* are essential. Neither the hazards associated with algorithms nor their boundaries are respected. A global race towards unbridled algorithmic dominance is prevented by shared standards on ethical AI, accountability, and transparency.

Essentially, the transition to smarter states is not a technical need but rather a political decision. Leadership, moral bravery, and democratic vision are required to ensure that states grow more just, compassionate, and legitimate as they become more intelligent.

6.7. The Revolution in Public Administration Motivated by AI

Public administration is undergoing a fundamental shift as a result of artificial intelligence, which is changing how governments make decisions, plan, and provide services. *Public institutions are transitioning from slow, paper-based bureaucracy to data-driven, flexible, and citizen-focused administration as a result of this revolution.*

The automation of regular administrative operations is at the heart of this revolution. Permits, licenses, tax returns, and benefit applications are now processed by AI algorithms faster than any human bureaucracy. AI-powered tax systems, for instance, can significantly cut down on processing time and administrative backlogs by automatically evaluating returns, identifying discrepancies, and issuing refunds.

The function of civil servants is also being redefined by AI. *Public officials are increasingly concentrating on policy design, oversight, and sophisticated case management rather than time spent on monotonous jobs.* In actuality, a welfare officer might use AI to pre-screen applications while employing expert judgement to deal with unique or delicate situations.

The emergence of predictive public administration is another significant change. AI allows for forecast and prevention, so governments no longer wait for issues to arise. Predictive analytics, for example, can predict hospital overcrowding, unemployment spikes, and infrastructure problems, enabling preventative measures that save lives and money.

Citizen-centered and individualised public administration is emerging. Instead of using one-size-fits-all methods, AI enables governments to customise services depending on individual needs.

Without requiring repeated applications, digital government systems can automatically inform residents about services they are eligible for, such as health checks or education funding.

In the public sector, AI is also improving accountability and performance management. Managers can spot inefficiencies, corruption risks, or underperforming departments by using algorithms that track service delivery indicators in real time. Instead of a rule-bound bureaucratic culture, this fosters one that is results-oriented.

But administrative power is also changing as a result of this change. Public management is becoming more technocratic as choices rely more and more on data systems and algorithms. Because of this, maintaining democratic control requires ethical scrutiny, openness, and civil service training.

In conclusion, intelligent systems that learn, adapt, and react instantly take the place of inflexible bureaucracy in the AI-driven revolution in public administration. When properly managed, it preserves the human judgement that characterises lawful public power while making the state a more intelligent service provider—faster, more equitable, and more responsive.

6.8. Transitioning from Bureaucracy to "Smart Bureaucracy"

A change from strict, rule-bound administration to intelligent, flexible, and technologically enhanced government is represented by the transition to smart bureaucracy. *Instead of doing away with bureaucracy, it modernises it so that it can operate efficiently in a complex, data-rich society.*

Paper-based processes, lengthy approval chains, and uniform application of standardised procedures—often irrelevant of context—are characteristics of traditional bureaucracy. *Digitally connected technologies that simplify processes and lessen administrative friction take the place of these inefficiencies in smart bureaucracy.*

For instance, *an AI-enabled one-stop digital portal can automatically verify paperwork, evaluate compliance, and grant approvals in place of a citizen visiting several agencies to obtain a business licence.*

Process automation with supervision is a hallmark of smart bureaucracy. Algorithms conduct routine and repetitive activities like data entry, form verification, and compliance checks, while civil servants monitor results and step in in complicated or unusual situations. This guarantees effectiveness without compromising responsibility.

Additionally, smart bureaucracy is responsive and data-aware. In order to find bottlenecks, delays, or service breakdowns, AI systems continuously examine operational data. Instead of waiting for yearly audits, the technology may identify the problem in real time if permit approvals in a certain area are often delayed.

Intelligence-driven rule flexibility is another significant change. Laws stay the same, but how they are applied becomes increasingly context-specific. *AI enables officials to exercise discretion within the bounds of the law by highlighting situations in which stringent rule enforcement may result in unfair outcomes, such as rejecting emergency help due to small documentation gaps.*

Smart bureaucracy is based on interoperability and system integration. Data is securely shared between government agencies, minimising duplication and inconsistencies. Instead of being disjointed, a citizen's interactions with social services, the health system, and the tax authority become seamless.

Above all, intelligent bureaucracy prioritises the citizen experience. Chatbots, automatic notifications, and AI-powered interfaces keep residents updated throughout the entire process, turning the government from an opaque authority into a service provider that is easily accessible.

Smart bureaucracy is essentially a combination of human judgement and machine efficiency. It integrates intelligence, speed, and adaptability while maintaining the stability, legality, and order of traditional bureaucracy, resulting in a public administration that is not only effective but also equitable, transparent, and sensitive to the actual demands of the populace.

6.9. Predictive Governance: Resolving Problems Before They Occur

Predictive governance is a clear change from reactive to proactive statecraft. *Governments employ AI and sophisticated analytics to foresee risks, trends, and social pressures, enabling early, focused response, rather than reacting to crises after damage has been done.*

Predictive governance is fundamentally based on the identification of patterns in massive datasets. Artificial Intelligence (AI) systems can detect early warning signs that are not evident to traditional policymakers by examining economic indicators, demographic trends, climate data, migration patterns, and social behaviour. *For instance, an imminent food-security crisis can be predicted months in advance when growing food costs are paired with meteorological information and migration trends.*

By monitoring hospital admissions, pharmacy sales, and movement data, predictive models in public health can predict disease outbreaks. Before hospitals are overburdened, this allows governments to pre-position medical supplies, send out health staff, and issue targeted public advisories.

By examining tax records, market trends, and sectoral performance, AI can predict business failures or increases in unemployment in economic and social policies. Then, before social unrest or widespread poverty arises, governments can implement retraining programs, targeted subsidies, or fiscal changes.

Infrastructure management and public safety are also transformed by predictive governance. *Traffic accidents, criminal hotspots, and infrastructure failures like power outages or bridge collapses can all be predicted by algorithms.* In order to save lives and public resources, emergency reactions are replaced by preventive maintenance and planned policing.

Predictive governance is particularly effective in managing climate change and disasters. By predicting floods, droughts, or wildfires, AI-driven climate models might facilitate early evacuations, adaptive farming recommendations, and financing for disaster risk reduction, so transforming disaster management into risk management.

Predictive governance, however, necessitates political discernment and ethical constraint. Risk prediction shouldn't turn into pre-emptive punishment or profiling. Forecasting crime trends, for instance, should direct community investment and prevention rather than serve as justification for monitoring or repression.

In the end, predictive governance gives the state foresight, which is the most precious and uncommon political commodity. It allows governments to safeguard individuals proactively, govern more wisely, and replace crisis politics with strategic, forward-thinking leadership when paired with accountability, transparency, and human oversight.

6.10. AI in Policy Design and Impact Assessment

By helping governments to transition from assumption-based policymaking to evidence-driven, forward-looking governance, AI is revolutionising effect assessment and policy creation. *Policymakers can now simulate, test, and improve policies before to implementation rather than depending just on expert opinion or historical precedent.*

In order to forecast how proposed policies would impact various population groups, Artificial Intelligence (AI) models examine enormous datasets, including economic indicators, demographic trends, behavioural data, and past policy outcomes. For instance, governments can utilise AI simulations to evaluate the effects of raising gasoline taxes on low-income households, rural communities, inflation, and transportation expenses before making changes that lessen social suffering.

Stress testing and scenario modelling are also made possible by AI. Within minutes, policymakers can investigate a number of "what-if" scenarios, including population increase, climate catastrophes, and economic shocks. Education ministries, for example, can model how curriculum revisions or changes in school funding will impact teacher demand, enrolment, and long-term workforce capabilities.

AI aids in identifying unforeseen implications in regulatory design. Algorithms can forecast pricing distortions, business closures, and compliance costs by analysing market data and regulation texts. This enables governments to create more intelligent laws that accomplish societal objectives without impeding creativity.

By emphasising distributional consequences, AI further promotes inclusive policy design. AI may demonstrate how policies impact women, youth, small enterprises, or vulnerable populations differentially rather than treating residents as a monolithic group, allowing for fairer decision-making.

AI significantly improves policy input and ongoing development. Real-time data streams enable computers to track results and suggest modifications after a policy is put into place. A social protection program, for instance, can be dynamically adjusted in response to shifting economic situations.

AI does not, however, take the place of political judgement. Public participation, democratic legitimacy, and ethical principles are still crucial. AI offers insight and accuracy, but people set the objectives, principles, and compromises.

AI-powered impact assessment and policy design essentially transform government into a learning system that anticipates outcomes, reduces harm, and creates more intelligent, equitable, and resilient policies.

6.11. Independent Public Services and Digital Government

The state's transition from a centralised, paper-based authority to a networked, technologically enabled service provider is symbolised by digital government. It transforms governance by increasing efficiency while preserving institutional autonomy and public trust when paired with autonomous public services.

Fundamentally, AI, data platforms, and interoperable technologies are used by digital government to provide services in a seamless manner. Instead of navigating several ministries, citizens can access social services, healthcare, taxes, licensing, and education through consolidated digital portals. To cut down on delays, mistakes, and corruption, for instance, a citizen asking for social assistance can be instantly connected to employment databases, tax records, and civil registration.

AI makes it possible to provide public services around-the-clock via chatbots, virtual assistants, and automated workflows. Fairness and accessibility are increased since routine interactions like scheduling appointments, monitoring applications, or requesting certificates are no longer dependent on office hours or personal ties.

Digital revolution greatly benefits independent public services, including public broadcasters, central banks, statistics agencies, electoral commissions, and regulators. By lessening political meddling in daily decisions, AI enhances their operational independence. An AI-driven election registration, for example, might restrict potential for manipulation by automatically identifying duplicate or ineligible voters based on objective criteria.

Additionally, digital tools improve the transparency and legitimacy of institutions. In order to enable people and oversight authorities to confirm performance, independent agencies can provide real-time data dashboards, audit trails, and algorithmic reports. For instance, a statistics office that uses AI to process census data can produce results more quickly and accurately without sacrificing methodological neutrality.

Standardisation and consistency are important benefits as well. Algorithms enable independent organisations fairly enforce legislation by applying rules consistently across circumstances. AI, for instance, can be used by a competition authority to continuously monitor markets and identify anti-competitive behaviour without the need for political pressure.

Digital independence, however, needs to be protected. If algorithms are politically controlled in terms of their design, data access, or monitoring, they may become tools of control. Therefore, maintaining autonomy requires strict legal requirements, open algorithm design, and external audits.

In conclusion, digital government makes the state more effective, unbiased, and reliable when it is combined with independent public services. It guarantees that public power is used through clear processes rather than partisan or personal influence, isolates service delivery from political discretion, and fortifies institutional independence.

6.12. AI in National Security and Public Safety

AI is becoming more and more important to national security and public safety, changing how governments respond to emergencies, prevent threats, and uphold law and order. AI makes it possible for governments to function quickly, accurately, and strategically by evaluating large datasets, identifying trends, and facilitating quick decision-making.

Predictive policing algorithms are used in crime prevention to predict possible criminal activity by analysing past crime data, social behaviour, and geographic patterns. AI systems, for instance, can predict areas where traffic infractions or burglaries are likely to occur, enabling law enforcement to deploy patrols proactively rather than reactively.

AI is used in counterterrorism to keep an eye on financial transactions, travel patterns, and digital interactions in order to identify possible threats. In addition to lowering the need for labour-intensive surveillance, algorithms can identify questionable activity or networks, assisting intelligence services in taking action before attacks happen.

AI also helps with immigration management and border security. Faster and more accurate identity checks at airports, ports, and land borders are made possible by facial recognition, biometric verification, and pattern analysis, which boost productivity while upholding national security standards.

AI systems in cybersecurity automatically react to malware, ransomware, or hacking attempts by identifying irregularities in real-time network traffic. Power grids, transportation systems, and communication networks are examples of national infrastructure that can be proactively defended against cyberattacks that could compromise public safety.

AI also helps with disaster management and emergency response. When floods, wildfires, or epidemics are predicted using predictive models, first responders and security personnel can strategically deploy resources to minimise damage and save lives. For example, in metropolitan areas vulnerable to earthquakes or flooding, AI-driven simulations can direct evacuation strategies.

However, there are moral and legal issues with using AI in public safety. If left unchecked, surveillance technologies, facial recognition, and predictive policing can violate people's privacy, disproportionately target marginalised groups, and foster a "pre-crime" mentality. It is crucial to guarantee supervision, responsibility, and conformity to human rights norms.

AI essentially turns reactive law enforcement into predictive governance, strengthening states' proactive ability to uphold security and public safety. When used properly, it protects civil liberties and the rule of law while bolstering national resilience.

6.13. Smart Cities: The AI-Powered Governance Model

AI-powered governance is best illustrated by smart cities, which show how technology can produce effective, sustainable, and citizen-focused urban settings. They function as living laboratories where AI combines infrastructure management, policy implementation, and public services into a coherent, intelligent system.

Data-driven urban management is the foundation of smart cities. Real-time data on traffic, energy use, garbage, water supply, and public safety is gathered by sensors, Internet of Things devices, and digital platforms. This data is processed by AI systems to improve city operations. For instance, predictive maintenance notifies authorities of malfunctioning infrastructure prior to accidents, while smart traffic systems dynamically modify signal timing to lessen traffic and pollution.

In order to optimise routes, schedules, and capacity in public transportation, AI-powered platforms examine commuter patterns and fleet performance. While cities attain more sustainable mobility, citizens gain from shorter wait times, cheaper prices, and improved connectivity.

Another distinguishing feature is the management of energy and resources. AI is used by smart grids to reduce waste, incorporate renewable energy sources, and balance supply and demand. Based on occupancy and consumption trends, buildings can automatically modify their water, heating, and lighting systems.

Additionally, smart cities improve emergency response and public safety. During emergencies, AI surveillance systems monitor high-risk locations, identify anomalies, and coordinate emergency services. Predictive flood models, for instance, can initiate early alerts that direct the deployment of first responders and evacuation routes.

Additionally, citizen engagement is changed. Residents can report problems, access services, and receive notifications using digital platforms, which creates a feedback loop that allows governance to adjust to the requirements of its population.

Additionally, AI can use social sentiment analysis to pinpoint issues or discontent, allowing for more responsive policymaking.

However, there are moral and political issues with smart cities. While algorithmic decision-making may unintentionally exacerbate inequality if it is not carefully handled, massive data collecting poses privacy concerns. To stop abuse, inclusive design, strong cybersecurity, and transparent governance are essential.

The future of AI-powered governance is essentially modelled by smart cities, which are responsive, predictive, efficient, and integrated. They show how algorithms, sensors, and human supervision may work together to build smarter urban settings that are also more resilient, sustainable, and habitable.

6.14. AI for Transparency and Anti-Corruption

AI is becoming a potent weapon to fight corruption and improve governmental openness. AI improves accountability, lowers the possibility of misuse, and increases public confidence in institutions by automating monitoring, analysing complex data, and identifying abnormalities.

Financial supervision is one important use. In order to identify anomalies like inflated bills, duplicate payments, or fraudulent activities, Artificial Intelligence algorithms can examine government budgets, procurement contracts, and spending data. Predictive models, for instance, can identify procurement bids that differ from market standards, assisting anti-corruption organisations in their investigations before money is embezzled.

AI-driven pattern identification is beneficial for public contract monitoring. Systems are able to monitor contractor performance, deadlines, and deliverables, pointing out delays, overspending, or poor quality work. This guarantees the completion of public initiatives.

AI also improves reporting and protection for whistle-blowers. In order to ensure that actionable information reaches authorities quickly while protecting informants, platforms can anonymise submissions, classify complaints, and prioritise investigations depending on severity or danger.

Another important effect is the transparency of policymaking. AI-powered dashboards can provide citizens with real-time access to government data, including spending, public service delivery, and regulatory decisions. Visual analytics, for example, may show which areas get the greatest public funds, allowing the media and civil society to hold policymakers responsible.

AI also makes risk prediction and avoidance easier. AI systems may predict weaknesses and advice governments on preventive actions by examining past patterns of financial flows, political networks, and corruption. This allows governance to transition from reactive investigations to proactive integrity management.

However, data integrity and ethical supervision are necessary when using AI to combat corruption. Because algorithms are only as trustworthy as the data they evaluate, incomplete or biased datasets may incorrectly detect hazards or unfairly single out certain people. To guarantee justice, transparent procedures and human scrutiny are essential.

AI essentially improves accountability tools, enabling governments to identify wrongdoing more quickly, enforce regulations more consistently, and increase transparency in public operations—laying the groundwork for a more moral and reliable state.

6.15. The Algorithmic State: Benefits and Risks

The term "*Algorithmic State*" describes a kind of governance where Artificial Intelligence (AI) and automated technologies are crucial to decision-making, the execution of policies, and the provision of public services. Although it has many benefits, there are also considerable hazards that need to be carefully considered.

Benefits

1. **Efficiency and Speed:** Algorithms enable quick decision-making by processing enormous volumes of data significantly more quickly than people. AI, for instance, can maximise the distribution of resources in times of crisis, like when a pandemic strikes and medical supplies need to be distributed.
2. **Consistency and Objectivity:** By applying rules consistently, algorithmic decision-making lessens the impact of political favouritism or personal prejudice. AI can guarantee that benefits are distributed equitably in welfare programs according to predetermined eligibility requirements.
3. **Predictive and Preventive Capacity:** The algorithmic state has the ability to foresee problems before they arise. Economic forecasting, catastrophe management, and predictive policing enable governments to take proactive rather than reactive measures.
4. **Transparency and Accountability (Potentially):** People can understand how judgements are made when algorithms are auditable and explicable, which can boost confidence. AI dashboards that are accessible to the public, for example, can display the effectiveness of social programs.

5. **Cost Reduction and Resource Optimisation:** By lowering administrative overhead, automation enables governments to reallocate human resources to high-value, strategic projects.

Risks:

1. **Loss of Human Judgement and Empathy:** Algorithms are incapable of comprehending compassion, ethics, or context. AI-only governance has the risk of becoming inflexible, dehumanising, and treating unusual circumstances harshly.
2. **Discrimination and Bias:** AI systems pick up prejudices from past data. Without proper planning, they could target marginalised groups in the welfare, judicial, or policing systems, perpetuating social injustices.
3. **Transparency Gaps:** A lot of AI systems function as "black boxes." Accountability gaps may result from citizens' ignorance of how decisions impacting their lives are made.
4. **Privacy and Surveillance Risks:** An algorithmic state requires a large amount of data. Without protections, this could result in invasive surveillance that undermines civil freedoms.
5. **Concentration of Power and Political Misuse:** Algorithmic governance can be used as a weapon for authoritarian goals such selective law enforcement, election manipulation, and the repression of opposition.
6. **Systemic Vulnerabilities:** AI systems are susceptible to hacking, misuse, or unforeseen repercussions, which could result in significant disruptions to vital services.

Essentially, the algorithmic state presents enormous ethical, social, and political concerns along with hitherto unheard-of efficiency, foresight, and justice possibilities. Its success hinges on striking a balance between automation and human monitoring, accountability, transparency, and strong ethical frameworks—making sure that technology advances society rather than taking the place of democratic judgement.

6.16. AI Systems + Human Leaders: The Future

AI will not replace people in governance; rather, intelligent computers will support human leadership in cooperative systems. This synergy blends the judgement, ethics, and empathy that only humans can offer with the speed, analytical capacity, and predictive powers of AI.

AI serves as a tool for decision assistance in such a paradigm. *To make well-informed policy decisions, leaders can use scenario modelling, predictive analytics, and real-time data.* For instance, AI can forecast outcomes, optimise resource allocation, and simulate various response plans during a natural disaster, while human leaders make the final decisions based on social, ethical, and political factors.

Accountability and moral guidance are guaranteed by human oversight. While AI can identify hazards, spot irregularities, or forecast economic trends, humans set priorities, balance trade-offs, and take into account values that algorithms are unable to measure. This avoids the rigorous rule-following or depersonalisation that can result from pure automation.

This partnership enhances public engagement and policy design. While leaders interpret these findings in light of public opinion, legal frameworks, and ethical norms, AI may identify citizen demands, foresee policy implications, and reveal inequities. Services that combine data-driven accuracy with human comprehension are efficient and equitable for citizens.

Transparency, explainable AI, and ongoing audits all incorporate checks and balances. While AI outputs are examined for bias, mistakes, or abuse, leaders are still responsible for their decisions. Both the efficacy of governance and democratic legitimacy are strengthened by this hybrid strategy.

Lastly, this collaboration promotes proactive and flexible governance. While leaders adjust policies dynamically, led by human judgement but informed by AI insights, predictive systems assist governments in anticipating disasters, such as public health emergencies, economic shocks, or climate concerns.

In short, the future state is a collaborative governance environment rather than one that is exclusively algorithmic or human. While humans make sure that leadership stays moral, responsible, and sensitive to the social and moral aspects of public life, AI enhances human potential to enable better, quicker, and more responsive governance.

The next stage of intelligent, citizen-centered governance is represented by this synergy.

6.17. Conclusion: Reimagined AI Is Changing the Laws of Governance

Artificial Intelligence is changing the fundamental ideas, procedures, and opportunities of governance itself; it is more than just a tool for governments. As states use AI to analyse massive datasets, forecast crises, optimise resources, and provide citizen-centric services with previously unheard-of speed and precision, the conventional rules of bureaucracy, policy-making, and public administration are being rewritten.

Three key aspects of governance are transformed by reimagined AI. It allows for anticipatory decision-making, to start. Predictive models enable governments to anticipate social, economic, and environmental issues and take proactive measures, eliminating the need for them to respond to catastrophes. Second, it promotes data-driven efficiency and fairness by streamlining public services, identifying anomalies, and enforcing regulations consistently while lowering the possibility of bias or corruption. Third, it enables responsive, adaptive governance, in which administration and policy continuously learn from real-time feedback, resulting in a state that changes in tandem with the needs of its people.

However, there are hazards associated with this change. *If left unchecked, AI has the potential to erode accountability, increase bias, concentrate power, and violate privacy. Despite its efficiency, the algorithmic state is only as moral as the people who create, manage, and direct it.* Using AI's enormous potential without sacrificing human judgement, democratic principles, or moral obligation is a challenge for contemporary administration.

The future of government ultimately rests in a cooperative ecosystem of human leaders and AI systems, with humans contributing insight, ethics, and responsibility and computers offering foresight, accuracy, and scalability. The laws of government are being rewritten by reimagined AI, but whether this new era results in more intelligent, equitable, and resilient states or a technocratic system detached from human values will depend on the decisions made by leaders, legislators, and citizens.

In this revolutionary era, government is about predicting, adapting, and morally leading society through a world that is becoming more and more characterised by data, algorithms, and intelligent systems. It is no longer only about upholding order.

Today's laws are written in part with a digital pen, but the hand that writes them must still be human.

Chapter 7: AI and Public Opinion: Comprehending the Nation's Views

Overview

Political fate has always been influenced by public opinion.
Kings sought advice from experts.
Polls were analysed by Presidents.
Foot soldiers were sent by the Parties to "*feel the ground*."
However, the *Landscape has drastically shifted* since then.
The new interpreter of national sentiment is *Artificial Intelligence (AI)*.
AI analyses people's emotions, predicts their thoughts, and reveals what they are reluctant to speak.
It does more than merely assess what people say.
This is a significant change in politics.
It signifies a change in the way leaders perceive, interact with, and impact the cultures they oversee.
The new science of AI-driven public opinion analysis is examined in this chapter along with its consequences for democracy, power, and political leadership.

Elections, policy choices, and national goals have all been influenced by public opinion, which has long been the lifeblood of democracy. *In the past, surveys, focus groups, and opinion polls were used by governments and political parties to determine public sentiment.* However, the accuracy, speed, and size of these techniques are constrained.

Artificial Intelligence (AI) has changed this environment in the twenty-first century. With the ability to analyse millions of social media posts, news stories, online forums, and citizen input at previously unheard-of speeds, governments and organisations may now track public mood in real time.

AI forecasts public opinion rather than merely measuring it. It can identify new social issues, identify possible catastrophes, and even predict election results. This chapter examines how AI captures a country's thoughts, as well as its advantages, drawbacks, moral dilemmas, and expanding influence on governance.

7.1. The Development of Analysis of Public Opinion

Over time, public opinion measurement has undergone significant change:

- **Early Techniques**: Small surveys or interviews were used for polling in the early 20th century. For instance, sample bias caused the Literary Digest to notoriously predict the 1936 U.S. presidential election incorrectly. Their survey, which was carried out by telephone respondents and magazine subscribers, disregarded the opinions of the general population and disproportionately represented richer Americans.
- **Modern Techniques:** With large datasets and sophisticated analytics, AI now enhances conventional polling. Rich data sources include citizen forums, internet petitions, government service reviews, and social media platforms. This data can be analysed by AI algorithms in a matter of seconds, revealing patterns that would take weeks for human analysts to identify.
- **Example:** AI tracked public opinion regarding lockdown procedures, vaccine hesitancy, and disinformation during the COVID-19 pandemic by analysing social media and search data. This allowed governments to quickly modify their communication plans.

7.2. AI Instruments for Gauging Public Opinion

AI is capable of comprehending citizens' ideas thanks to a number of tools:

7.2.1. **Analysis of Sentiment**

Text from news stories, social media posts, and comments is scanned by algorithms to determine whether it is neutral, negative, or positive.

- **Example:** As an illustration, AI-powered sentiment analysis of Twitter posts during the 2019 Indian elections enabled political parties to assess popular reaction to policy announcements and campaign speeches.

7.2.2. **Topic Modelling**

To find popular subjects, AI groups discussions around recurring themes.

- **Example:** AI was utilised in Kenya throughout the 2022 general elections to spot new issues like water scarcity and job development, assisting NGOs and decision-makers in concentrating on the pressing demands of the populace.

7.2.3. **Social Media Opinion Mining**

Social media sites like Facebook, Twitter, and TikTok function as public journals in real time.

- **Case Study:** AI monitored voter concerns by examining millions of tweets throughout the 2020 U.S. elections. Days or weeks prior to mainstream media coverage, trends such as "postal voting security" and "COVID-19 economic impact" were recognised.

7.2.4. **Predictive Analytics**

AI forecasts how the public would respond to proposed laws or political initiatives.

- **Example:** The UK government employed Artificial Intelligence (AI) to predict public opinion on Brexit negotiations by examining news, social media, and online forums to identify areas of public support or fear.

7.2.5. **Voice and Video Analysis**

AI examines the motions, tone, and facial expressions in town halls and public speeches.

- **Example:** Local governments in Singapore tested Artificial Intelligence (AI) techniques to evaluate citizens' happiness and emotional response to PSAs during town hall meetings.

7.3. Data Sources and Their Difficulties

AI uses a variety of datasets, but each has drawbacks:

7.3.1. **Social Networks**

- **Strength:** Offers vast, real-time insights.
- **Limitation:** Bots and trolls can skew statistics, thus it might not accurately reflect all demographics.
- **Example:** Automated bots disseminated false information during the 2016 U.S. elections, underscoring the dangers of depending only on emotion on social media.

7.3.2. **Polls and Surveys**

- AI enhances survey analysis by addressing sampling biases and spotting hidden trends in responses.
- **Example:** The Pew Research Centre employed AI to modify survey demographic weighting for the 2020 elections, improving forecasts.

7.3.3. **Opinion Pieces And News Media**

- AI is able to identify public opinion, tone, and framing bias in traditional media.
- **Example:** AI monitored media sentiment during the 2019 Hong Kong protests to comprehend public opinion both locally and globally.

7.3.4. **Public Records and Comments from Citizens**

- To find reoccurring problems, complaints, petitions, and civic engagement platforms are examined.

- **Example:** The city of Barcelona employed AI to evaluate public grievances over urban infrastructure and direct focused enhancements.

7.3.5. **AI Case Studies in Public Opinion**

- **Election Predictions**: AI systems examined millions of news articles and social media posts in order to forecast the results of the 2019 general elections in India. The system was successful in identifying the constituencies that were most affected by problems such as agricultural distress and unemployment.
- **Monitoring initiative Acceptance:** AI monitored public responses to a new school reform initiative in South Korea. The Ministry of Education was able to pinpoint areas that required improved communication or policy changes thanks to negative sentiment spikes.
- **Crisis Management:** AI systems tracked social media during Hurricane Harvey in 2017 to pinpoint areas in critical need of assistance, enabling emergency services to react more quickly.
- **Corporate Public Sentiment:** AI's cross-sector adaptability is demonstrated by businesses like Starbucks and Amazon, which utilise it to measure consumer sentiment and enhance customer service outside of governments.

7.4. AI's Advantages for Public Opinion Analysis

By offering scale, speed, and precision well beyond conventional techniques like surveys and focus groups, artificial intelligence offers substantial advantages in comprehending and interpreting public opinion.

First, *AI is capable of processing enormous amounts of data in real time, extracting insights from online forums, news sites, social media, and digital government portals.* Instead of depending on delayed or static snapshots, this enables political actors and policymakers to monitor popular mood as it changes.

Second, *AI improves analysis's complexity and subtlety.* In a variety of languages and cultural situations, *Natural Language Processing* (NLP) algorithms are able to identify feelings, tone, framing, and underlying issues. This makes it easier to discern between superficial approval and more profound fears, expectations, or mistrust.

Third, *AI enhances the capacity for prediction.* AI models can predict changes in public opinion, possible unrest, or support for particular policies by seeing patterns and trends. This allows for proactive rather than reactive government.

Finally, when correctly developed, *AI lowers bias and expense in opinion analysis, providing more inclusive insights by collecting perspectives that traditional polling frequently misses.* In the digital age, ethical use of AI makes it a potent instrument for responsive democratic engagement and evidence-based governance.

7.5. Dangers, Prejudices, and Moral Issues

AI presents significant ethical, social, and moral concerns that need to be properly addressed, even though technology offers potent tools for political engagement and public opinion study:

- **Risks:** AI has the potential to be used as a weapon to sway public opinion, disseminate false information, or magnify contentious stories. Deepfake technologies, micro-targeted messaging, and automated content distribution can sway elections, polarise communities, or erode public confidence in institutions. AI may enable widespread monitoring, censorship, and the repression of opposition in authoritarian settings.
- **Prejudices:** The impartiality of AI systems depends on the data and algorithms that power them. Systematic discrimination that marginalises particular groups or distorts public opinion can result from historical biases, inadequate datasets, or faulty training procedures. When AI influences resource allocation or policy decisions, this is especially problematic.
- **Moral Concerns:** The application of AI in political settings calls into question consent, responsibility, and transparency. People might not be aware that their information is being examined or utilised to sway their actions. The balance between effective governance and manipulation, privacy versus the public benefit, and automated decision-making versus human monitoring all provide ethical challenges.

In conclusion, AI presents concerns of abuse, ingrained bias, and moral compromise even as it provides previously unheard-of insight and efficiency in public opinion analysis. To guarantee that AI supports democracy rather than threatens it, responsible deployment necessitates stringent ethical frameworks, transparency, human monitoring, and legislative protections.

Example: Cambridge Analytica's use of Facebook data to micro-target voters during the 2016 U.S. elections illustrated the potential and moral dilemmas of Artificial Intelligence in public perception.

7.6. Combining Human Understanding with AI

Combining human judgement with algorithmic knowledge is necessary to maximise the advantages of AI in political and public opinion studies. AI is excellent at analysing large datasets, spotting patterns, and forecasting trends, but it is devoid of contextual awareness, moral judgement, and the complexity of human experience.

AI-generated insights benefit from human interpretative abilities, empathy, and moral judgement. For instance, human analysts might evaluate cultural context, historical variables, and socio-political dynamics to determine the proper response, but an AI model might identify growing dissatisfaction in social media mood. This guarantees that computerised forecasts or statistical correlations are not the only factors influencing policy decisions.

Risks like bias, misinterpretation, and an excessive dependence on algorithms are also reduced when AI and human expertise are combined. To uphold accountability, justice, and moral integrity, humans can audit AI outputs, question presumptions, and exercise oversight.

In actuality, this hybrid method produces a feedback loop in which AI provides humans with data-driven insights, humans analyse and act upon those insights, and the results gradually improve AI models. Societies may use AI for more responsive, inclusive, and ethically sound governance by utilising both computer capacity and human judgement.

7.7. AI's Potential in Public View

Artificial intelligence has the ability to significantly alter how the general public views, engages with, and takes part in governance. AI may improve accessibility, transparency, and citizen participation when used properly, resulting in a society that is more knowledgeable and adaptable.

AI-powered systems can offer real-time insights into societal trends, government performance, and policy outcomes, allowing citizens to swiftly comprehend complicated issues. By making information more personalised and accessible, chatbots, digital assistants, and interactive dashboards enable people to participate actively in civic life and make educated decisions.

Furthermore, through sentiment analysis, participatory platforms, and prediction tools that enable citizens to participate in decision-making processes, AI can promote wider engagement. Governments can better address the needs and preferences of their communities by conducting a large-scale analysis of public feedback.

However, trust, responsibility, and openness have an impact on how the public views AI. Building confidence requires explicit information about AI's role in decision-making, ethical use, and visible protections. AI has the ability to increase democracy, better governance, and improve the general interaction between citizens and the state when certain conditions are met, placing technology as a collaborator in public empowerment rather than a manipulative tool.

7.8. Conclusion

Artificial intelligence is drastically changing public opinion analysis, political participation, and governance. For governments, political players, and citizens alike, its capacity to analyse large amounts of data, identify patterns, and forecast results presents previously unheard-of prospects. When used appropriately, AI can improve democratic responsiveness, citizen participation, and policy-making, resulting in more effective and evidence-based governance.

AI also presents serious moral, societal, and ethical issues. Over-reliance on algorithms, bias, manipulation, and privacy intrusions can erode public confidence, skew public opinion, and jeopardise democratic ideals. These dangers underscore the vital necessity of ethical frameworks, human oversight, accountability, and openness.

The ability of society to successfully integrate human judgement with computational power, striking a balance between innovation and accountability, will determine the future of AI in politics. By achieving this, AI can transform from an instrument of persuasion into a force for inclusive, knowledgeable, and moral governance, creating a robust, adaptable, and participative political landscape in the era of algorithms.

Chapter 8: The Future Brain: Interfaces, Implants, and Political Cognitive Enhancement

8.1. Overview: Neurotechnology and Politics

Innovation is nothing new in the political sphere, but the next frontier lies not in AI analytics or campaign tactics but in the human mind. Brain-computer interfaces (BCIs), neural implants, and cognitive improvement tools are examples of *neurotechnology* that has the potential to completely transform the way political leaders think, make decisions, and exert influence.

Imagine a world in which a politician could decipher complicated legislation in a matter of seconds, anticipate the public's reaction instinctively, or converse with advisors with ease using just their thoughts.

The relationship between politics and new neuro-technologies—such as brain-computer interfaces (BCIs), neural implants, and cognitive enhancement tools—is discussed in this section.

It emphasises how new technologies could revolutionise political leadership by facilitating quicker decision-making, improved strategic thinking, and a more intuitive grasp of public opinion. In essence, it lays the groundwork for a future in which political power is derived not only from knowledge or influence but also from the capacities of the human brain, enhanced and linked by cutting-edge technology.

8.2. Political Decision-Making with Brain-Computer Interfaces (BCIs)

This section examines how political leadership could be transformed by *Brain-Computer Interfaces* (BCIs), which *are gadgets that directly link the human brain to computers or Artificial Intelligence systems.* By converting brain activity into useful insights, BCIs can help executives understand complex data, model policy outcomes, and make quick decisions.

Additionally, they make it possible for decision-makers to collaborate telepathically, which facilitates smooth coordination and communication under duress. In essence, political decision-making might be accelerated, more accurate, and thoroughly informed by real-time data thanks to BCIs.

These days, brain-computer interactions are not just science fiction. Medical and military applications are being researched for devices that read brain activity and convert it into useful data. BCIs could speed up decision-making in politics by allowing leaders to "think" through scenarios using AI-assisted cognitive simulations:

- **Improve Situational Awareness:** Politicians might virtually instantaneously identify trends, crises, or public opinion by directly integrating real-time data streams into brain perception.
- **Facilitate Telepathic Collaboration**: By eschewing conventional communication channels, groups of advisers or leaders could exchange ideas directly.

Case Study: Neuralink researchers have shown that primates can operate robotic limbs just by thinking. Apply this to governance: a future cabinet may reduce bureaucratic lag by using mental instructions to change intricate policy models in real time.

8.3. Augmented Intelligence and Cognitive Improvement

This section looks at how technologies that improve cognitive abilities—such as brain stimulation, Nootropics, or neural implants—can change political leadership. *By improving memory, reasoning, creativity, and emotional intelligence, cognitive enhancement could help politicians forecast social and economic trends, handle massive datasets quickly, and create policies that more successfully connect with the public.* By fusing human intuition with AI-powered insights, augmented intelligence produces leaders who are more strategically aware and quick thinkers.

Essentially, this combination of human and Artificial Intelligence has the potential to completely reinvent what it means to be a capable, progressive political leader.

Beyond interfaces, cognitive augmentation through implants, neurostimulation, or Nootropics may enhance emotional intelligence, memory, reasoning, and creativity.

This could show up in politics as:

- **Hyper-Analytical Leadership**: Leaders who can quickly analyse large datasets and see patterns that are not obvious through traditional analysis.
- **Emotionally Intelligent Persuasion**: Politicians may be able to better grasp public opinion by using enhanced empathy circuits to craft policies that appeal to a broad audience.
- **Strategic Foresight:** By enhancing predictive modelling, neural augmentation may be able to foresee social, economic, and geopolitical events with previously unheard-of precision.

Example: Consider a politician who has a neural implant that allows them to see in real time how a new tax policy will affect different demographic groups.

8.4. Implications for Ethics and Democracy

The ethical and political issues raised by neurotechnology in governance are examined in this section. *Although brain implants and cognitive upgrades have the potential to increase a leader's intelligence and effectiveness, they also pose significant questions around equity, manipulation, and transparency.* For instance, social inequality may worsen and a cognitive elite may emerge if only political leaders have access to these improvements.

Additionally, there's a chance of controlling or influencing thoughts, which compromises the ability to make decisions on one's own. Lastly, voters might find it difficult to believe that augmented leaders are making decisions independently of AI or implanted technologies. This section highlights the need for cautious ethical frameworks to safeguard democracy and citizen rights when incorporating neurotechnology into politics.

Neurotechnology presents significant ethical concerns despite its enormous potential:

- **Equity**: *Will political elites be the only ones who benefit from cognitive augmentation, increasing the divide between citizens and leaders?*
- **Manipulation:** *Could implants allow for delicate manipulation of thought processes or compulsion for political purposes?*
- **Transparency**: *How can voters make sure that politicians are not overly dependent on AI-brain interfaces and are instead making their own decisions?*

Case Study: In order to enhance decision-making in high-stress governmental positions, China carried out initial study in 2024 on the use of non-invasive neuro stimulation. Critics cautioned about possible state overreach into private thought, even though the results were encouraging.

8.5. Interface Politics: Combining Humans and Technology

This section examines how direct brain interfaces, which link human thoughts to AI systems and to one another, could revolutionise political processes. Real-time leadership cooperation, neuro-targeted citizen communication, and even immediate democratic involvement through brain-linked voting or feedback could all be made possible by such interfaces.

Political decision-making could become quicker, more accurate, and more sensitive to public opinion by combining cognitive with artificial intelligence. It also calls into question the boundaries of human-machine integration in governance, consent, and privacy.

Direct brain interfaces may also change policy formulation and political campaigning:

- **Neuro-Targeted Messaging**: Politicians might use aggregated neural data to craft messages that appeal to citizens' subconscious preferences in place of generic campaigns.
- **Direct Democracy:** A fluid, real-time democratic process might be created by allowing citizens with brain interfaces to take part in instant voting or policy feedback.
- **Crisis Response:** Neural-linked decision networks could coordinate government and emergency services during crises, maximising neural-cognitive reactions.

Example: A neural dashboard would enable a president to "feel" the sentiment of the country in social, economic, and environmental domains and make dynamic policy adjustments.

8.6. Dangers and Prospects

This section looks at the possible risks and hypothetical consequences of incorporating neurotechnology into politics. While cognitive enhancers and brain implants can improve decision-making, they also put leaders at risk for manipulation, mental overload, and cognitive hacking. Fairness and democracy could be threatened by the emergence of a cognitive elite in which only politicians with advanced skills can effectively compete.

Future possibilities include both authoritarian abuse, where improved cognition concentrates authority and diminishes accountability, and ultra-efficient, data-driven governance. The section highlights the necessity of managing these technologies properly in order to strike a balance between innovation and democratic and ethical protections.

There are risks associated with combining politics and brain technology:

- **Cognitive Hacking:** Cyberattacks that target brain implants run the risk of altering mental processes or disclosing private data.
- **Mental Overload:** The brain may get overloaded by constant neuronal connectivity, which could result in mental exhaustion, burnout, or decision paralysis.
- **Authoritarian Abuse:** By centralising power through the employment of mind-enhancing technologies, governments may create a cognitive elite that is not subject to accountability.

Analysis of Scenarios Imagine a future election in which candidates have neural implants to enhance their performance.

Fairness and the future of democratic choice may be called into question if those without access are cognitively outcompeted.

8.7. The Path Ahead: Power, Ethics, and Innovation in Balance

Unmatched efficiency, insight, and competence are promised by neurotechnology in politics, but only if it is directed by robust ethical frameworks and fair access.

In addition to navigating public opinion and policy, the next generation of political leaders may also have to deal with their own enhanced cognitive abilities.

Using these capabilities to benefit citizens rather than just outwitting rivals will be the difficult part. Circuits and synapses may be just as important to governance's future as laws and policies.

Chapter 9: Artificial Intelligence and Intellectual Property Law: Who Controls the Algorithmic Mind?

Overview

A crucial dilemma arises as AI starts to actively participate in political strategy, governance, and even policy creation: *Who owns the ideas produced by AI?*

This is a significant political and social issue with ramifications for innovation, leadership, and democracy itself. It is not only a technical or legal subject.

Traditional IP divisions are blurred by AI systems. Questions can be divided into multiple categories:

- *When output is created with little to no human creative input, who, if anyone, may be considered an "Author" or "Inventor"?*
- *Who is the owner of the model and its results?*
- *What rights are retained by the owners of the training data, and what restrictions apply when it is aggregated or scraped?*
- *How should intellectual property systems be changed to strike a balance between democratic oversight, creator rights, innovation incentives, and transparency?*

This chapter provides case studies (actual trends + illustrative hypotheticals), breaks down legal doctrines (copyright, patents, trade secrets, database rights), looks at how courts and regulators are responding, and suggests contracts and policy choices for an equitable path ahead.

9.1. Key Legal Building Components (A Plain-Language Primer)

Knowing the fundamental legal principles governing AI models, their application, and the results they produce is essential to comprehending the legal environment around AI. This is a condensed explanation:

9.1.1. Rights to Intellectual Property (IP):

- Safeguard intellectual property, such as software, designs, inventions, and written works.
- Text, music, and art are examples of expressive works that are protected by copyright.
- New technical solutions or inventions are protected by patents.
- Logos and brands are protected by trademarks.
- When it comes to AI, intellectual property concerns centre on who owns the model and the creations it generates.

9.1.2. **Contracts Licensing:**

- Establish legal guidelines for the use of AI tools and software, frequently outlining ownership of outputs, rights to commercial usage, and limitations.
- In order to prevent infringement, users must abide by these terms.

9.1.3. **Data Protection and Privacy Laws:**

- These regulate the collection, storage, and processing of sensitive or personal data.

- When AI uses data for analysis or training, laws like the EU's GDPR or other national rules guarantee that people's rights are upheld.

9.1.4. **Contract Law:**

- Contracts can define ownership, responsibility, and duties for AI-generated outputs. They also cover agreements between parties using or accessing AI.

9.1.5. **Liability and Accountability**:

- Generally, individuals or organisations in charge of the AI are held liable when it does harm, makes mistakes, or violates rights.

9.1.6. **Ethics and Regulatory Compliance**:

- In high-risk industries like healthcare, banking, or criminal justice, legal frameworks increasingly demand that AI systems be transparent, equitable, and explicable.

To put it briefly, *AI legislation is based on who owns the technology and its outputs, who can use it, how data is handled, and who bears responsibility for its effects.* Anyone developing, implementing, or overseeing AI technology must comprehend these fundamental components.

9.2. Who is the owner of both the model and the products AI produces?

Ownership of an AI model and the goods it produces is a complicated legal and moral issue that is influenced by jurisdictional laws, contracts, and intellectual property law:

9.2.1. **Ownership of the AI Model**:

Unless otherwise noted in a contract or license, the organisation or person that created, taught, and maintained the system is usually the owner of an AI model.

- Since work produced while an individual is employed is regarded as "Work for Hire," the corporation typically retains ownership of AI developed by its employees.
- Ownership of models created by independent researchers or open-source groups may be divided or controlled by license contracts.

9.2.2. **Ownership of AI-Generated Products (Outputs)**:

Generally speaking, as long as the outputs adhere to the conditions of the AI's license, the creator or user of the AI system that produces content is the owner of the rights to the outputs.

- In certain jurisdictions, copyright protection requires human authorship, which can make claims more difficult when AI functions independently.
- Businesses, especially in commercial settings, might claim

ownership by entering into contracts that state that outputs produced with their instruments are their property.

9.2.3. **Issues and Difficulties:**

- The ownership of an AI model's outputs may be legally disputed if it was trained on proprietary or copyrighted data.
- Concerns are raised on whether AI can be regarded as an "author" or whether ownership is always transferred to humans who oversee or manage the AI.
- Licensing conditions from AI providers (like OpenAI and Google) frequently specify usage rights and limitations, which have a direct impact on who is permitted to use or market the AI's products.

9.2.4. **Useful Patterns**

- To control models, large companies rely on trade secrets and licensing.
- With open-source approaches, the focus is on license compliance.
- In their Terms of Service (ToS), service models (API access) negotiate output licensing.

In conclusion, ownership usually belongs to the person or organisation managing and running the AI, but since legal frameworks are still developing, it is crucial to take contracts, licensing, and intellectual property regulations into account when figuring out who has rights over AI models and their outputs.

9.3. "The Human Touch," Authorship, And Inventiveness

The degree of human involvement in directing, moulding, or producing the finished output determines the concept of authorship and originality in AI-generated works. Although AI is capable of producing writing, art, code, or designs on its own, existing legal systems typically acknowledge humans, not computers, as the owners of intellectual property rights.

- **The Human Touch:** A human's creative decisions, intent, and guidance when utilising AI are referred to as the "human touch." For instance, a person may choose prompts, modify outputs, or mix AI-generated content in novel ways. This human input is essential for proving authorship because copyright and patent rules usually need a verifiable human component in production.
- **Authorship (Copyright):** Since AI lacks legal personality and intent, it cannot be acknowledged as an author in the majority of states.

This approach guarantees accountability, attribution, and conformity with conventional intellectual property systems. Humans who exercise control, judgement, and creativity over AI outputs are typically considered the authors of the resulting work.

- **Inventorship (Patents):** Inventiveness is associated with a work's uniqueness and originality. Legal acknowledgement of ingenuity typically requires a human mind to conceptualise, refine, and steer the outcome, even though AI can provide innovative combinations or solutions.

- In patent law, for instance, courts and patent offices are progressively making it clear that, even in cases where artificial intelligence played a major role in the creative process, only human inventors are entitled to credit.

The *legislation nevertheless places a strong emphasis on the human component of creativity and innovation, even when AI essentially serves as a tool or collaborator*. In an AI-driven society, the human touch establishes authorship, safeguards creativity, and guarantees that intellectual property rights continue to be significant and enforceable.

9.4. Training Data: Legal Vs Illegal Scraping

AI models rely on training data, but the methods used to gather it can give rise to significant legal concerns. Responsible AI development requires an understanding of the distinction between legal and illicit data scraping:

Legal Scraping:

It *entails collecting information in a manner that conforms to terms-of-service, copyright, and privacy regulations.*

- Using publicly accessible datasets that are specifically licensed for commercial or academic usage is one example.
- Gathering information with users' or data owners' express consent.
- Making use of content that is accessible under Creative Commons or other permissive licenses.
- *Why?* By ensuring that AI developers respect individual privacy and intellectual property rights, legal scraping lowers the possibility of legal action or regulatory fines.

Illegal Scraping:

When data is gathered without authorisation or in contravention of legal or commercial obligations, it is known as *Illegal Scraping.*

- Content extraction from websites that violates their terms of service is one example.
- Using copyrighted content for AI training without a license.
- Gathering personal information without authorisation or in contravention of privacy regulations like GDPR.

- Illegal scraping may tarnish the *legitimacy of AI-generated outputs and expose developers to legal action, regulatory fines, and reputational harm.*

Points of Legal Friction:

- Owners of copyrights assert that extensive text, image, and code scraping violates their rights.
- Because models encode patterns rather than exact replicas, AI businesses contend that scraping for training falls outside of reproduction rights or qualifies as fair use or essential input.

High-Level Real-World Trend:

- A number of lawsuits alleging illegal copying and scraping have been brought against prominent AI companies by authors, artists, and publishers. For the time being, litigation is influencing practice more than doctrine; results are inconsistent and jurisdiction-specific.

Key Takeaway: The source, ownership, and licensing of training data must be thoroughly examined by AI engineers. Not only is ethical and legal compliance necessary for compliance with regulations, but it also safeguards the legitimacy and profitability of AI models.

9.5. Open-Source and Licensing: Who Grants Authorisation and Under What Conditions?

Open-source software and artificial intelligence are governed by particular licenses that specify how technology may be disseminated, altered, and used. Deploying AI in a way that is both ethical and lawful requires an understanding of who gives permission and the terms involved.

Who Issues Permission:

- Individuals, groups, or organisations that maintain the code base and enforce adherence to the license terms may oversee open-source projects.
- The original developers or copyright holders of the AI model or software usually provide authorisation through licensing agreements.
- Implicit authorisation is frequently obtained by license acceptance, whereby the user consents to the terms by using the program.

Typical Licensing Requirements:

1. **Permissive licenses (such as Apache 2.0 and MIT):**

- Permit distribution, alteration, and use with few limitations.
- Frequently call for giving credit to the original authors.
- Fit for both academic and commercial endeavours.

1. **Copyleft licenses**, such as the GPL:

- Only permit distribution and alteration when derivative works are made available under the same license.
- To avoid proprietary lock-in, make sure AI ideas stay open and shareable.

1. **Proprietary Or Custom Licenses:**

- Commercial use, dissemination, or modification may be restricted by proprietary or custom licenses.
- Frequently contain clauses that outline output ownership, liability, and approved uses.

Important things to keep in mind are:

- Licensing establishes who can claim rights over AI-generated outputs and under what circumstances they can be commercialised; users must read and abide by licensing terms to prevent infringement.
- Even open-source AI can be prohibited from using certain data for model training or from using its results in industries that are subject to regulations.

In conclusion, requirements differ based on the type of license, and authorisation comes from the license holder rather than the AI itself. Comprehending these regulations guarantees that the advancement and use of AI remain lawful, moral, and economically feasible.

9.6. Notable Flashpoints Include Enforcement, Litigation, And Regulatory Responses.

A number of legal and regulatory flashpoints have surfaced as AI use picks up speed, influencing how governments, businesses, and users manage risk, accountability, and compliance.

9.6.1. **Enforcement:**

- Regulators throughout the world are starting to keep an eye on AI use to make sure it complies with ethical, intellectual property, and data protection regulations.
- When businesses break privacy laws, copyright regulations, or safety standards, enforcement may take the form of fines, penalties, or limitations on the use of AI.

Example: The EU's AI Act suggests a risk-based framework that places stringent requirements on high-risk AI applications like vital infrastructure and biometric identity.

9.6.2. **Litigation:**

- Ownership of AI outputs, copyright violations, and unapproved data scraping are becoming more common legal issues.
- Courts are being challenged to determine whether works created by AI may be protected by copyright and who is responsible when AI infringes or causes harm.

Example: As an illustration of the conflict between innovation and intellectual property protection, cases have contested the unapproved use of copyrighted content for AI model training.

9.6.3. **Regulatory Reactions:**

- With an emphasis on safety, accountability, and transparency, governments are creating rules, regulations, and laws to control the development and application of AI.
- These reactions range greatly, from lax frameworks that promote innovation (such as U.S. guidelines for AI in government) to stringent, legally binding laws that prioritise morality and human rights (such as the EU AI Act).
- To make sure AI systems adhere to moral and legal requirements, regulatory agencies are also looking at auditing, certification, and risk assessment procedures.

Key Takeaway: As AI develops quickly, it creates a dynamic legal environment where legislation, enforcement, and litigation come together. To reduce legal risks and guarantee responsible AI adoption, developers, users, and legislators must continue to be watchful, striking a balance between innovation, responsibility, and public confidence.

High-Level Summary (Do Not State Particular Court Rulings Unless Independently Verified): The DABUS-style inventor question and copyright claims made by authors and artists over scraped training data have been routinely challenged by courts and patent offices in recent years.

The recurring pattern is cautious conservatism: *while challenges over data use are still settling and influencing practice, authorities choose human-centered legal categories and have rejected or restricted rights for wholly machine-generated output.*

(Publishers, legislators, and attorneys should keep a careful eye on these cases since they quickly alter the legal environment.)

9.7. Case Studies: Actual Patterns and Speculative Examples

Case Study A: "DABUS and the Inventor Question" (Overview of Trends)

Context: An AI system generated a technical concept on its own. The AI was listed as an inventor in patent applications submitted by its developer. Several jurisdictions' patent offices and courts insisted on a human inventor name and rejected non-human inventors.

Lesson: Businesses that use Artificial Intelligence (AI) to generate inventions must either guarantee human engagement and attribution or advocate for legislative reform, as current patent regimes are built for human Inventorship.

Case Study B: "Writers vs. Model Trainer" (Illustrative Litigation Pattern)

Context (Trend): big AI corporations have been sued by groups of writers and artists who claim that the indiscriminate scraping of books, articles, and photos to train big language and image models constitutes copyright infringement.

Hypothetical Ruling: Depending on the jurisdiction and evidence, a court may decide that extensive verbatim copying is infringement, but it may also decide that some forms of transformative training are fair use.

Lesson: Businesses should develop opt-out/ compensation methods for producers, obtain licenses when feasible, and record the provenance of data.

Case study C: "Start-Up Licensing Error" (Real-World Example)

Scenario: A start-up uses a third-party dataset with ambiguous license terms to refine an open-source model. The dataset's creator files a breach lawsuit against the start-up after it commercialises an app.

Result and Lesson: Use warranties and representations in acquisition contracts; incorporate indemnity from dataset vendors; and always clarify dataset licensing.

Case Study D: "Platform ToS and User Ownership" (Creator-Platform Dynamics)

Scenario: An online platform provides makers with AI tools. The ToS of the platform asserts extensive rights over produced outputs. Later, when creators wish to commercialise their results, they run into license issues.

Lesson: Policymakers may need to control consumer-friendly default settings; creators should negotiate explicit IP agreements or steer clear of platforms that assert ownership.

9.8. Practical Provisions and Contracts (Templates for Practitioners)

9.8.1. Employment And Contractor Agreements (AI Work)

- **Assignment Clause:** Employer/Client is the owner of all inventions, models, and outputs produced during employment or engagement.
- **Moral Rights Waiver:** The creator forfeits moral rights over generated works to the extent that it is allowed.
- **Data Provenance Warranty:** The contractor guarantees that data used for training and fine-tuning does not violate intellectual property rights of third parties.

9.8.2. Model/Data Acquisition Contract (For Businesses Purchasing Datasets)

- **License Grant:** Clearly defined rights to use for commercial exploitation, transfer/sub-licensing, and model training.
- **Warranties and Representations:** No third-party claims are made; the seller indicates legitimate ownership and the right to license data.
- **Indemnity & Cap:** The seller protects the customer from intellectual property lawsuits resulting from the dataset; the cap is based on the purchase price.
- **Audit And Provenance:** The ability to keep provenance logs and audit dataset sources.

9.8.3. AI output SaaS/API Terms (for platforms)

- **Output Ownership Clause**: Specify whether and under what circumstances customers own outputs (e.g., stewardship vs. assignment).
- **Options With And Without Attribution:** Policies and optional attribution tags for derivative works.
- **Model Training Clause**: Indicate whether user-supplied data can be used for additional model training (opt-in vs. opt-out).
- **Liability and Indemnity:** Specify who is responsible for allegations of infringement resulting from outputs.

9.9. Suggested Legal Reforms and Policy Options

9.9.1. Practical and Short-Term Solutions

1. Promote voluntary licensing frameworks between AI labs and creator organisations by establishing clear safe-harbour licensing regimes.
2. Standardised metadata for dataset contents and licenses—training-data registries and provenance standards.
3. Disclosure and transparency regulations mandate that AI creators notify downstream licensees and buyers of important data sources and model capabilities.

9.9.2. Medium-Term Changes to the Law

1. **Sui Generis AI Rights:** Take into account limited, time-bound legal frameworks that protect original creators while rewarding model developers (e.g., mandatory licensing with royalty shares).
2. **Authorship Thresholds**: legal guidelines (such as a codified "creative contribution" test) that specify what constitutes human authorship for works helped by artificial intelligence.
3. **Inventorship Reform:** amend patent law to allow for AI-assisted inventions with precise ownership and assignment guidelines.

9.9.3. Long-Term Institutional Modifications

- Public-interest data trusts, which oversee the ethical reuse of specific public datasets.

- AI IP tribunals or specialised chambers—to develop technical know-how and reliable precedents.

9.10. Implications for Democracy and Ethics

There are significant ramifications for democracy and moral judgement when AI is included into politics and government. AI poses serious threats to democratic norms, accountability, and moral standards even while technology can improve efficiency, policy analysis, and citizen involvement.

9.10.1. **Consequences for Democracy**:

- **Impact on Public Opinion**: AI has the ability to undermine fair elections and informed decision-making by micro-targeting voters, manipulating emotion, and shaping narratives.
- **Power Concentration**: Asymmetries of power can result from nations or businesses controlling cutting-edge AI systems dominating political discourse and policy impact.
- **Accountability and Transparency**: Automated decision-making may make it difficult to determine who is in charge of making policy decisions, undermining established democratic oversight procedures.
- **Inclusion and Engagement**: On the other hand, by identifying underserved communities, analysing extensive comments, and supporting evidence-based policymaking, AI can increase citizen engagement.

9.10.2. **Ethical Implications:**

- **Bias and Fairness**: AI systems have the potential to replicate or magnify social biases, which could result in unfair outcomes in the areas of healthcare, justice, policing, and resource allocation.

- **Privacy and Consent**: Individual rights and informed consent must be respected while collecting and analysing personal data.
- **Autonomy and Human Judgement**: Relying too much on AI could reduce human judgement and moral accountability.
- **Manipulation and Misinformation**: When AI is used to trick people, spread lies, or take advantage of cognitive weaknesses, ethical issues come up.

Key Takeaway: The use of AI in politics and governance necessitates a delicate balancing act between democratic principles and technological efficiency. To guarantee that AI enhances rather than diminishes democracy, justice, and human dignity, ethical frameworks, transparency, human oversight, and regulatory protections are crucial.

9.11. Stakeholder Checklist

Several stakeholders must actively participate in and oversee the deployment of AI in order for it to be both responsible and effective. Governments, developers, organisations, and people can use this checklist as a useful foundation to make sure AI is applied morally, legally, and openly:

9.11.1. **Governments and Regulators:**

- Create *precise AI regulations and guidelines* that address data use, privacy, and intellectual property.
- For high-stakes AI applications, *put risk assessment and auditing procedures in place.*
- *Keep an eye on compliance and impose sanctions* for abuse or violations.
- *Encourage digital literacy and public awareness* of AI's place in society.

9.11.2. **Start-Ups, AI Companies & Developers:**

- Make sure AI systems are understandable and transparent.
- Make use of training data that is ethically and legally sourced.
- Include measurements for inclusion, fairness, and bias detection in the model's design.
- Clearly state who owns, licenses, and is responsible for AI outputs.
- Create a dataset-clearance function that logs permissions, licenses, and sources.
- For risky datasets, get releases or use express licensing.
- Make advantage of contractual provisions to guarantee

output ownership and properly allocate Inventorship.

9.11.3. **Academics and Civil Society:**

- Conduct independent studies and audits to assess the effects of AI.
- Promote moral and human-centered AI regulations.
- Inform people on the potential, constraints, and dangers of AI.

9.11.4. **End-Users and Citizens:**

- When working with AI systems, citizens and end users should be aware of terms of use, data rights, and privacy protections.
- Evaluate AI-generated information critically for dependability, bias, and correctness.
- Take part in feedback systems to affect the deployment and governance of AI.

9.11.5. **International and Multilateral Organisations**:

- Organise ethical frameworks and cross-border AI norms.
- Encourage the exchange of knowledge and the development of AI governance capabilities in poor countries.
- Keep an eye on and reduce algorithmic power disparities between dependent countries and AI superpowers.

9.11.6. For Artists, Authors, and Developers:

- Maintain the original works' provenance and provide a clear license.

- Don't give up all rights; instead, use explicit contracts with platforms.
- If at all possible, register works and record human input into AI-assisted outputs.

9.11.7. For Decision-Makers

- Demand basic transparency (disclosures of training data).
- Promote uniform dataset licenses and dispute settlement procedures.
- Take into account test mandatory licensing programs that pay royalties for content that is scraped.

9.11.8. **For Solicitors**:

- When purchasing datasets or models, draft strong indemnities, guarantees, and representations.
- Provide clients with guidance on jurisdictional variations and developing case law (copyright registrations, patent offices).
- Incorporate documentation requirements to bolster defence tactics (e.g., proof of transformative training).

Diagram: Ethical AI Governance Stakeholders Checklist

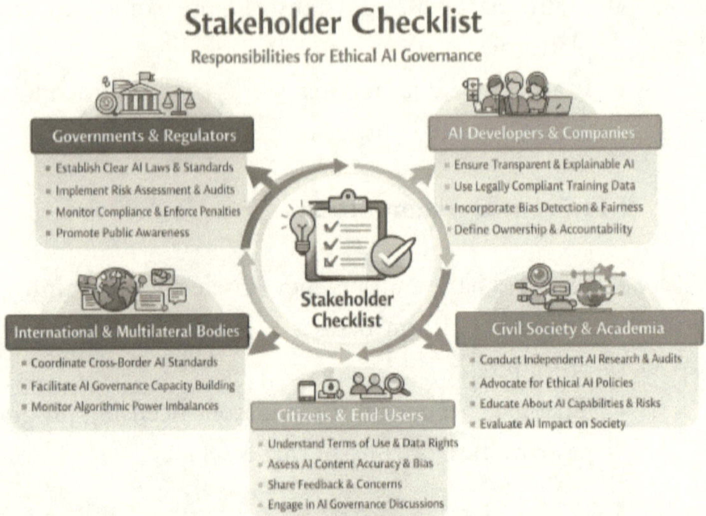

Figure 11: Ethical AI Governance Stakeholders Checklist

Figure 11: *Illustrates Stakeholders' check list, itemising responsibilities for ethical AI governance.*

Key Takeaway: The main lesson is that accountability for AI is a shared duty. To guarantee AI benefits, all stakeholders must actively participate in ethical supervision, legal compliance, and ongoing assessment.

9.12. A Useful Guide to Arranging an IP-First AI Project

By ensuring that intellectual property (IP) considerations are incorporated from the beginning of an AI project, an IP-first strategy protects ownership, legal compliance, and commercialisation possibilities. Here is a useful, step-by-step tutorial:

9.12.1. **Establish Goals and Scope**:

- Clearly state the AI project's goals, intended uses, and planned results.
- As this influences IP strategy, ascertain if the initiative is commercial, research, or hybrid.

9.12.2. **Examine Current IP:**

- Determine which pre-existing models, code, datasets, or third-party tools will be utilised.
- To prevent infringement, verify patent, copyright, and licensing status.
- Keep track of all intellectual property contributions made by workers or colleagues.

9.12.3. **Determine Ownership and Rights:**

- Determine who is the owner of the AI model, training set, and produced results.
- To make IP assignment clear, draft agreements for workers, contractors, or partners.
- Define the derivative's conditions.

9.12.4. **Ensure Ethical and Legal Data Use:**

- Confirm that all training data is sourced properly, adhering to privacy, copyright, and licensing regulations.
- Steer clear of unlawful scraping and make sure licenses for public usage or consent are acquired.

9.12.5. **Put The Licensing Plan Into Action**:

- Choose a suitable license and decide if the AI will be proprietary, open-source, or hybrid.
- Make sure users understand their responsibilities, limitations, and permissions.

9.12.6. **Safeguard Innovations:**

- Take into account obtaining a patent for new algorithms, procedures, or uses.
- For proprietary methods or datasets that are not patentable, use trade secrets.

9.12.7. **Keep an Eye on Risk and Compliance:**

- Set up IP monitoring, documentation, and auditing systems.
- Keep abreast on AI-related legal and regulatory developments.

9.12.8. **Plan Commercialisation and Collaboration**:

- Create agreements with clients or partners to safeguard intellectual property while facilitating cooperation.
- Add clauses pertaining to revenue sharing and licensing

9.12.9. **Plan Cooperation and Commercialisation**:

- Create agreements with clients or partners to safeguard intellectual property while promoting cooperation.
- Add clauses pertaining to future invention rights, license fees, and income sharing.

Important Takeaway: Innovation, legal protection, and ethical responsibility are all balanced in an IP-first AI initiative. In an increasingly complicated AI environment, companies can protect their innovations, optimise value, and reduce operational and legal risks by incorporating IP considerations from the outset.

9.13. Concluding Scenarios: Three Futures and Their Implications for Politics

Three broad scenarios show potential futures and their political ramifications as AI continues to transform society, governance, and global power:

9.13.1. AI-Integrated Democracy:

- **Scenario:** Strong ethical monitoring is maintained while AI is fully utilised to improve public decision-making, policy formation, and citizen participation.
- **Consequences:**
    - Real-time insights into public demands are obtained by policymakers, enhancing responsive government.
    - Political procedures and elections become more open and inclusive.
    - Human oversight and legal protections reduce the possibility of bias and manipulation.
    - As AI serves citizens rather than control systems, political legitimacy and confidence are reinforced.

9.13.2. AI-Authoritarianism:

- **Situation**: AI is mostly used for political manipulation, social control, and surveillance, consolidating power in the hands of the state or powerful individuals.
- **Consequences:**
    - Governments are highly effective at anticipating, influencing, and stifling criticism.

  - As AI techniques are employed to support ruling parties or governments, political competition may wane.
  - Privacy, civil liberties, and democratic
  - Privacy, democratic procedures, and civil freedoms are jeopardised.
  - Algorithmically enforced power asymmetries result from citizens' diminished ability to influence policy.

9.13.3. **The World Of AI Fragmentation**:

- **Scenario**: AI superpowers rule the world, AI-dependent countries follow, and AI-invisible countries are marginalised due to uneven AI adoption.
- **Consequences:**
  - As superpowers establish regulations for trade, security, and information flows, international relations become extremely unequal.
  - It might be difficult for developing countries to keep control over political narratives and decision-making.
  - As AI-driven inequality exacerbates economic, technological, and political inequities, global governance concerns grow.
  - In order to prevent exploitation and war, international cooperation and regulation become essential.

Key Takeaway: How civilisations decide to manage, regulate, and integrate AI will have a greater impact on its political ramifications than the technology itself. To steer AI towards democratic empowerment rather than authoritarian control or global fragmentation, proactive ethical frameworks, human oversight, and inclusive policy design are crucial.

9.14. Concluding Remarks: Striking a Balance between Inventors, Creators, and the General Public

We are at a turning point in policy. AI compels us to decide whether to adapt current doctrine, create targeted new regimes, or leave allocation to contract and market power. IP law was designed for human creators. Every decision has political ramifications: *it determines who owns information, how powerful synthetic capacities are regulated in democracies, and who gains income from culture and creativity.*

Diagram: Striking a Balance – Innovation, Inventors and Public Good

Figure 12: Striking a Balance between Innovation, Inventors and Public Good

Figure 12*: Illustrates how Legal and Ethical Frameworks can be used to ensure AI-powered politics strike a balance between Innovation, Rights and Public good.*

The next five years will be essential in determining whether the "algorithmic mind" benefits society as a whole or concentrates its benefits in a few number of hands for writers, legislators, and engineers who want to protect innovation and the public good.

Chapter 10: Ethical AI in Politics: Juggling Democracy, Power, and Responsibility

Overview

Politics is changing at a rate never seen before thanks to artificial intelligence. AI has a widespread impact on everything from elections to administration, public opinion analysis to cognitive enhancement. However, this enormous power comes with a crucial obligation: *making sure AI advances democracy rather than threatens it.*

In the Algorithmic Age, ethical AI is now essential for sustainable leadership. The concepts, difficulties, and structures required to responsibly regulate AI in political contexts are examined in this chapter.

This chapter also makes the case that whether AI is used as a weapon of empowerment or dominance will determine the future of democracy. Whether society approach an era of algorithmic enlightenment or algorithmic tyranny depends on the ethical regulation of political AI.

10.1. Power without Ethics is a Democratic Risk

There has never been a technology revolution that is changing politics as quickly as artificial intelligence. These days, *algorithms have an impact on how governments distribute resources, how leaders gauge public opinion, how campaigns mobilise voters, and how citizens obtain information*. Political authority is increasingly mediated by code, from AI-assisted policymaking and surveillance-enabled government to predictive analytics in elections.

However, history offers a harsh lesson: *abuse is inevitable when authority is exercised without moral restraint*. Unregulated AI runs the potential of undermining the fundamental tenets of democracy in politics, where legitimacy is based on consent, trust, and transparency. Therefore, ethical AI is a political imperative rather than a philosophical luxury.

Why Ethics Matter in Political AI

AI has the ability to:

- Impact elections;
- Mould public opinion;
- Direct policy decisions;
- Anticipate social catastrophes; and
- Enhance government operations.

Without moral protections, these capacities run the risk of:

- Citizens' manipulation;
- Privacy infractions;
- Algorithmic bias;
- Political elites' entrenchment; and
- A decline in public confidence in democratic institutions.

Ethical AI guarantees the responsible use of power and the preservation of public confidence.

AI systems function at scale, speed, and opacity in contrast to conventional political tools. Millions of lives can be suddenly impacted by their choices, frequently with no obvious accountability.

Important ethical dangers consist of:

- **Concentration of Power:** People who have access to data, computing power, and technical know-how—typically governmental institutions, big parties, or political elites—benefit from AI.
- **Opacity and Black-Box Decision-Making:** People are unable to contest decisions that they do not comprehend.
- **Manipulation of Public Opinion:** Micro-targeted communications can take advantage of psychological weaknesses and avoid logical discussion.
- **Behavioural Control and Surveillance:** Under the pretence of security, AI-driven surveillance might stifle dissent.
- **Automation of Bias:** Data-based historical disparities are enshrined into policy.

These concerns are increased in political circumstances because AI governs people rather than just markets.

10.2. Fundamentals of Ethical AI in Politics

Political AI must be governed by fundamental ethical concepts in order to maintain democratic integrity:

10.2.1. **Transparency**
People need to be aware of:

- ***When** AI is applied to political decision-making;*
- ***What** information the system uses;*
- ***How** results are produced.*

If governance is reduced to a mystery run by computers, a democracy cannot survive.

10.2.2. **Responsibility**

A human authority must always be in charge of AI-driven results. People have the power to hold algorithms accountable, punish them, or remove them from office.

The following questions should be addressed by clear accountability frameworks:

- *Who **created** the system?*
- *Who **gave their approval** for its use?*
- *Who **bears responsibility** for damage?*

10.2.3. **Equity and Non-discrimination**
Political AI cannot:

- Discriminate against minority groups;

- Strengthen racial or socioeconomic prejudices; or
- Prevent citizens from engaging in politics.

Continuous bias audits are necessary for ethical AI.

Inclusive datasets and ongoing bias assessments are necessary for ethical AI.

10.2.4. Human Oversight

- AI should support political judgement rather than take its place.
- Final decisions must continue to be made by humans, particularly those that impact rights, freedoms, or representation.

10.2.5. Limitation of Purpose and Proportionality

The employment of AI must be:

- Required for a justifiable political objective;
- Proportionate to the issue being resolved; and
- Restricted in scope and duration.

An algorithmic solution is not necessary for every political problem.

10.3. Ethical AI in Elections: Preserving Democracy

The ethical use of AI is no longer optional as technology becomes increasingly integrated into election processes, from media monitoring and results transmission to voter registration and campaign planning. It is essential to democratic systems' existence and legitimacy.

The term "Ethical AI in Elections" refers to *the development, implementation, and management of AI systems in ways that uphold human rights, safeguard democratic principles, and bolster rather than erode public confidence.*

The most delicate application of political AI is during elections. **Risks** include:

- AI-generated false information and deepfakes;
- Voter profiling and psychological manipulation;
- Suppression or distortion of political pluralism; and
- Unequal access to AI campaign tools.

Safeguards for Ethics

- AI-generated political content must be disclosed;
- Micro-targeting based on sensitive personal data must be limited;
- Campaign algorithms must be independently audited, and
- Equal-access regulations to stop electoral monopolies powered by AI.

Elections impacted by covert algorithms are now steered outcomes rather than free choices.

10.4. AI Ethics in Public Administration and Governance

AI ethics are becoming essential to legitimate, efficient, and democratic administration as governments use AI more and more to run public services, allocate resources, enforce laws, and make policy decisions. Since public administration has the ability to coerce citizens, unlike the private sector, unethical government AI systems can directly result in unfairness, exclusion, and a decline in public confidence in the government.

Efficiency is promised by AI, but efficiency without morality leads to technocratic dominance.

Possibilities include:

- Better service delivery and resource allocation;
- Automated oversight reduces corruption;
- Evidence-based policymaking.

Ethical Risks

- Loss Of Administrative Discretion And Compassion;
- Automated Exclusion Of Disadvantaged People; And
- Algorithmic denial of public services

"**Explainable Bureaucracy**"—*systems that provide human justifications for decisions*—is necessary for ethical governance.

Making sure that technology efficiency never takes precedence over human dignity, justice, and democratic accountability is the goal of AI ethics in public administration. AI has the potential to make states more intelligent, equitable, and responsive when it is used ethically. The state runs the risk of becoming an unaccountable machine when it is poorly run.

AI IN POLITICS: THE RISE OF ALGORITHMIC GOVERNANCE

Algorithms must continue to be the public's servants rather than its lords in democratic governance.

10.5. Security, Monitoring, and the Slippery Digital Authoritarianism's Slope

One of the most serious moral conundrums in politics is AI-driven monitoring.

Unchecked surveillance can:

- Criminalise dissent,
- Normalise constant monitoring,
- Stifle free expression and association, even when it is justified in the fight against crime and terrorism.

Judicial supervision, explicit legislative requirements, and stringent data retention restrictions are all necessary components of ethical boundaries. Autonomous civilian review organisations

Eventually, everything is under the power of a state that sees everything.

10.6. International Frameworks and New Standards

National governments alone cannot control ethical AI in politics. Important new strategies consist of:

- Algorithmic Impact Assessments (AIAs),
- International AI Ethics Charters,
- Human Rights-Based AI Governance, and
- Cross-border data governance agreements.

Geopolitical rivalry, however, runs the risk of producing an "AI ethics gap," in which authoritarian regimes weaponise AI more quickly than democracies control it.

10.7. Establishing Democratic AI Organisations

Institutional innovation, not merely regulation, is necessary for ethical AI.

- National AI Ethics Councils,
- Parliamentary AI Oversight Committees,
- Public Algorithm Registries, and
- Civic AI literacy initiatives, are among the suggested frameworks.

In the age of algorithms, democracy must change institutionally to stay relevant.

10.8. The Ethical Duty of Leadership in the Age of Algorithms

Leaders in politics have a historic obligation. Future generations will evaluate the governance of the technologies as well as their adoption.

- Transparency over secrecy;
- Restraint over temptation; and
- The public good over political advantage - are all necessary for ethical leadership in AI.

Ethics is strategy in the Age of Algorithms.

10.9. Conclusion: Democracy Is Designed, Not Accidental

Whether or not society are ready, artificial intelligence will influence politics. The question is whether AI will rule democratically, not if it will rule at all. The conscious decision to include democratic values into institutions, leadership culture, and code is known as ethical AI in politics.

AI turns into a tool of dominance in the absence of ethics. It becomes a force for responsibility, inclusivity, and group intelligence when ethics are involved. The algorithms that increasingly influence political reality will determine the future of democracy, not just at the polls.

Elections, government, public communication, and national security are already being influenced by artificial intelligence. Governments run the risk of losing institutional credibility, democratic legitimacy, and public confidence if they do not control political AI.

Ethical AI is becoming a governance necessity rather than a choice. To guarantee that AI enhances democratic systems rather than undermines those, policymakers must take proactive measures.

Chapter 11: Comparative Case Studies - US, China, and Russia on AI and Political Power

Overview: AI as a Novel Political Player

Artificial intelligence has subtly evolved from a technical support system to a key player in political influence, power, and governance. *AI is now influencing how political statements are created, how public opinion is tracked, how elections are contested, and how states project influence outside of their boundaries.* It is no longer limited to administrative efficiency or data analysis.

The integration of AI into the political ecosystems of three key global powers—China, Russia, and the United States—is examined in this chapter. Each reflects a unique approach of integrating AI and politics, influenced by institutional architecture, political culture, and strategic aims.

When taken as a whole, they show how AI is rethinking democracy, sovereignty, and geopolitical rivalry in the era of algorithms.

11.1. The US: AI in Democratic Defence and Election Competition

11.1.1. AI in Election Strategy and Political Campaigns

AI is now a potent instrument in American electoral politics, especially when it comes to voter engagement and campaign strategy. *AI-driven analytics are used by political parties and politicians to categorise voters, forecast electoral behaviour, tailor messaging, and maximise fundraising efforts.* In order to identify persuasive voters, assess issue salience by demographic group, and customise messaging across digital platforms, campaigns are depending more and more on machine learning models.

Campaign communication has been further revolutionised by generative AI. The speed and scope of political messaging have increased thanks to AI-assisted content creation, which includes anything from digital ads to draft speeches and policy announcements.

Although these tools increase productivity and competitiveness, they also raise moral questions about manipulation, misinformation and authenticity.

11.1.2. Debate on Deepfakes, Disclosure, and Regulation

Significant regulatory discussion has been sparked by the appearance of AI-generated deepfakes in US election campaigns. Voter deception and reputational damage are problems associated with the convincing misrepresentation of political actors in synthetic movies, photos, and audio recordings.

In response, state legislatures and regulatory bodies like the Federal Election Commission have started looking into transparency requirements for political content produced by AI. Policies requiring the labelling of synthetic media in political adverts have also been implemented by technology platforms.

These initiatives are representative of a larger conflict in liberal democracies: striking a balance between the right to free speech and the requirement to maintain electoral integrity.

11.1.3. AI for Election Security and Counter-Disinformation

AI protects American democratic systems in ways that go beyond campaigning. AI systems are used by government organisations and tech firms to track foreign-sponsored disinformation campaigns, identify bot networks, and detect coordinated inauthentic behaviour.

AI is being seen as a national security issue rather than just a communications problem, as evidenced by the sanctions placed on foreign actors who use AI to tamper with elections. In this situation, AI is a dual-purpose technology integrated into democratic governance that serves as both a threat vector and a protective tool.

Case Study A: AI-Generated Political Advertising

Example: Republican campaigns (RNC, NRSC) have issued AI-generated advertisements that construct political narratives using deepfakes and synthetic.

One such example is an AI video of Chuck Schumer making false claims about a government shutdown.

Context and Policy Reaction:

- The Federal Election Commission (FEC) is now investigating ways to control or mandate the disclosure of political information created by artificial intelligence in advertisements.
- A number of U.S. states, including Minnesota, Wisconsin, Arizona, and Florida, have passed or are proposing legislation requiring the labelling of AI-generated political advertisements or possibly making undeclared deepfakes illegal.
- Google and other tech companies require political advertisements to disclose any artificial material.

Key Insights: The U.S. debate emphasises the conflict between the rights to free expression and the negative effects of disinformation, with new legislation frameworks attempting to require transparency.

Case Study B: Foreign AI-Enhanced Disinformation against the U.S.

Example: The Centre for Geopolitical Expertise, a Russian-affiliated organisation, was sanctioned by the U.S. Treasury in January 2025 for utilising artificial intelligence (AI) techniques to create and spread widespread disinformation prior to the 2024 U.S. presidential election.

This disinformation included bogus reports about political personalities and edited films.

Impact: The operation created more than 100 fake news websites and disseminated content intended to sway voters' opinions and divide American viewers.

Key Takeaway: In an effort to circumvent moderation and sway public opinion in the United States, foreign state actors are utilising AI to create autonomous content networks.

Case Study C: Disinformation Waves and the Information Environment

Example: Following the murder of conservative activist Charlie Kirk, social media was flooded with thousands of unfounded allegations and conspiracies, which were exaggerated by China, Iran, and Russia.

Mechanism: This illustrates how foreign players and AI-enhanced networks can create thematic narratives around social events to distort public opinion.

Key Insights: In times of crisis, AI helps with both content production and the quick thematic amplification of polarising storylines.

11.2. China: The Use of AI in Ideological Governance

11.2.1. Centralised Narrative Control and AI

China offers a political AI model that is essentially different. The Chinese government incorporates AI into ideological control and narrative management instead of concentrating mostly on electoral competitiveness. In China, generative AI systems must support official stances on history, national identity, and sovereignty by conforming to state-approved political narratives.

Public discourse is guided by AI-driven content moderation and automatic censoring systems, which make sure that politically sensitive subjects are framed—or suppressed—in ways that align with official interests.

This strategy is part of a larger ideology that views AI not as a disruptive breakthrough but as a stabilising force that strengthens political order.

11.2.2. AI in Behavioural Management and Social Governance

AI is becoming more and more integrated into China's social government structure, going beyond information control. Authorities can monitor public attitude and identify possible causes of disturbance through AI-assisted surveillance, sentiment analysis, and predictive analytics.

These systems are frequently combined with administrative databases and digital identity infrastructures to provide a complete solution for managing big populations.

In this concept, anticipation and prevention are used in addition to laws and coercion to exert political power. Instead of using overt political action, AI becomes a silent administrator that shapes behaviour through data-driven governance.

11.2.3. Chinese Model Exportation

There are global ramifications to China's AI governance framework as well. Other governments, especially those in poorer nations, are progressively adopting aspects of this centralised, state-aligned AI approach through technological exports and collaborations.

This raises questions about the spread of digital authoritarianism around the world, as stability is prioritised over plurality through the employment of AI tools.

Case Study D: Multilingual Content Campaigns & "Spamouflage"

Example: In order to target worldwide audiences on issues impacting China's soft power, the Chinese state-affiliated Spamouflage operation deployed generative AI algorithms to produce text and social media postings in multiple languages (English, Chinese, Japanese, and Korean).

Application: AI helped investigate social trends and produce content that was shared on social media sites like Facebook, Medium, and X (Twitter) in order to mould positive narratives or soften criticism.

Key Takeaway: China's strategy employs AI to create multilingual, cross-platform content operations that combine automated volume with appealing messaging, frequently avoiding overt political statements but subtly influencing dialogue.

Case Study E: Synthetic Grassroots Personas and "Uncle Spam"

Example: In addition to using AI for messaging, Chinese actors also employed it to build logos, engagement histories, and fictitious grassroots organisations and personalities (such as "Veterans for Justice").

Strategies: These accounts then took part in divisive discussions on topics like social policy or tariffs, giving the appearance of widespread, natural public participation.

Key Takeaway: China's use of AI combines story transmission with synthetic persona engineering, a combination of social engineering and influence strategy that is uncommon at this scale.

11.3. Russia: The Use of AI in Asymmetric Political Warfare

11.3.1. Disinformation and Influence Operations Powered by AI

AI has mostly been adopted by Russia as a tool for asymmetric influence and information warfare. Artificial intelligence (AI) is used by Russian-affiliated actors to produce fake news pieces, replicate reputable media websites, fabricate social media personalities, and automate the spread of polarising narratives.

Russia's AI policy places more emphasis on external disruption than either China's or the US's concentration on internal control or electoral competitiveness. The goal is to polarise, confuse, and undermine confidence in democratic institutions rather than necessarily persuade.

11.3.2. Deepfake Warfare and Psychological Operations

Deepfakes produced by AI are an essential part of Russian political activities. Artificial audio and video recordings aimed at political leaders take advantage of feelings rather than reason. These efforts are intended to flood information surroundings, making it challenging for citizens to discern between fact and fiction.

This tactic is part of a larger Russian strategy that sees information as a battlefield. AI enables long-lasting impact with believable deniability by reducing the cost and expanding the scope of such operations.

11.3.3. Implications for Strategy

Russia's use of AI shows how open societies are susceptible to false information that is amplified by algorithms. It also heralds the start of a global information arms race powered by AI, in which nations vie not only for economic or military might but also for dominance in perception and narrative.

Case Study F: "Doppelgĩ" Disinformation Campaign

Example: The Russian-Affiliated Doppelgĩ® operation used generative AI to create and repost fake headlines, comments, and articles that imitated reputable Western media sources, frequently with pro-Moscow or anti-Western narratives. It targeted the US and Europe with localised misinformation and spoof outlets.

Key Takeaway: Russia has operationalised AI to mimic trust signals from Western media, reducing detection and increasing the legitimacy of misleading narratives.

Case Study G: Propaganda Associated with Russia and Storm-1516

Example: During elections, the group Storm-1516 (associated with Russian propaganda networks) disseminated fake allegations against American political personalities, including those about vice presidential nominees, using AI-generated actors, films, and made-up claims.

Strategies: The digital footprint of targeted disinformation was expanded by paid actors and fictitious personas.

Key Takeaway: For long-lasting effect, Russian operations combine AI content generation with human-moderated social engineering, which combines synthetic output with human editorial guidance.

Case Study H: AI-powered Bots in "Bad Grammar"

Example: Russian-affiliated "Bad Grammar" used AI-programmed bots to produce brief political remarks in both Russian and English on Telegram, which helped disseminate unfavourable stories about NATO, the United States, and Ukraine.

Note: Platform interventions were used to identify and stop this campaign.

Key Takeaway: State actors can grow propaganda-like interaction by strategically using AI to automate bots that provide political comments.

11.4. Comparative Evaluation: Three Political AI Models

Three different political AI paradigms are shown via a comparison analysis:

- **China** incorporates AI into centralised governance and ideological control, emphasising stability and narrative coherence;
- **Russia** weaponises AI for external influence and psychological disruption, taking advantage of openness in rival systems;
- **The United States** uses AI for electoral optimisation and democratic defence, constrained by legal norms and civil liberties.

Notwithstanding these variations, all three examples show how AI has permeated political power institutions, changing the way power is used and challenged.

Themes of Cross-Case Analysis

11.4.1. AI Boosts Scale and Reduces Production Costs

AI significantly lowers the work needed to create political content in all three scenarios:

- The extent of operations across platforms and languages is influenced by China and Russia.
- AI is used by US campaigns to produce communications and advertisements more quickly and affordably.

11.4.2. Dual-Use Nature

- AI is employed for threat modelling research and defence (detection, moderation) in addition to political influence and persuasion.

11.4.3. Ethical and Regulatory Reactions Lag

Regulations and governments find it difficult to keep up:

- There are growing federal and state initiatives in the US to mandate disclosures for AI advertisements.
- Malicious AI abuse is now being labelled, blocked, or sanctioned by tech platforms.
- China and Russia export message abroad and maintain narrative control at home, frequently avoiding open disclosures.

11.5. Implications for Governance and Policy

11.5.1. AI as Infrastructure for Politics

AI should now be viewed as a type of political infrastructure, similar to electoral laws, media systems, or diplomatic establishments. States with insufficient AI capabilities run the risk of becoming strategically vulnerable, while those that use AI carelessly run the risk of losing credibility.

11.5.2. Regulation, Ethics, and Trust

Transparency, accountability, and public trust are necessary for the effective governance of political AI. While under-regulation encourages manipulation and foreign meddling, overregulation may limit political expression. One of the most important governance issues of the twenty-first century is striking this equilibrium.

11.5.3. AI Literacy in Politics

To traverse a world full of artificial content, citizens, legislators, and electoral institutions need to become AI literate. Even well-crafted legislation may not be able to safeguard democratic processes in the absence of public comprehension.

11.6. Conclusion: The Algorithmic Rewriting of Power

In contemporary politics, artificial intelligence has emerged as a quiet but powerful influence. It influences how states compete internationally, how leaders communicate, and how societies are run—often without being directly visible to the public.

The key political question of the AI era is no more whether or whether AI will have an impact on government, but rather who will control it, under what conditions, and for what purpose.

This chapter illustrates how the answer to that question will impact not only policy discussions and election results, but also the future nature of democracy, sovereignty, and political power.

Chapter 12: AI and International Diplomacy: Algorithms in the Global Arena

12.1. Overview: The Algorithmic Era of Diplomacy

Information—who has it, how fast it spreads, and how well it is interpreted—has long influenced diplomacy. Artificial intelligence has emerged as the most potent tool ever developed for handling diplomatic data in the twenty-first century. *These days, algorithms examine diplomatic cables, forecast geopolitical threats, simulate the results of negotiations, identify disinformation efforts, and even recommend foreign policy reactions.*

From intuition-driven diplomacy to data-augmented statecraft, this is a momentous shift. *AI changes how power is viewed, used, and negotiated on the international scene, but it does not replace diplomats.* Countries that become proficient in algorithmic diplomacy gain influence, speed, and strategic insight. Those who don't run the risk of being diplomatically blind.

These days, *AI is integrated into international organisations, intelligence services, foreign ministries, embassies, and multilateral negotiating platforms.* Consequently, diplomacy is increasingly carried out across servers, models, and neural networks rather than just across tables.

Figure: The Evolution of Diplomacy – From Human Judgement to Algorithmic Statecraft

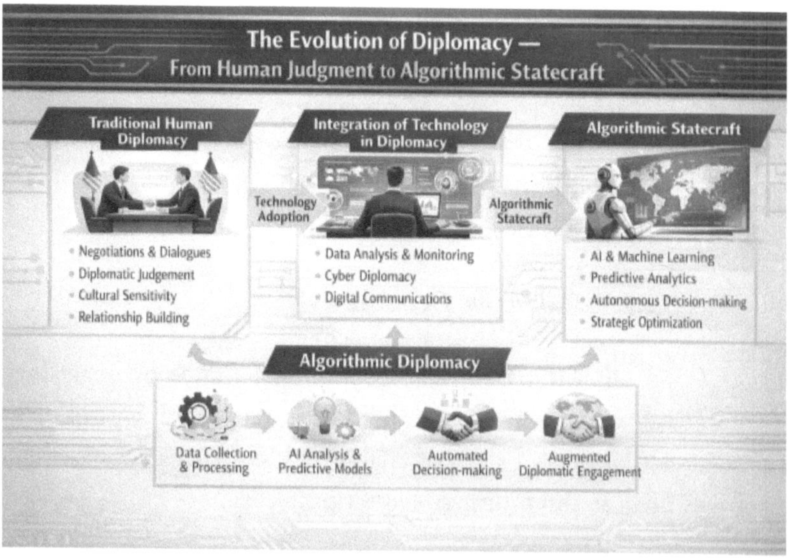

Figure 13: The Evolution of Diplomacy – From Human Judgement to Algorithmic Statecraft

Figure 13: *Shows how diplomacy has evolved from interaction based on intuition to statecraft boosted by algorithms. AI is rapidly influencing perception, timing, and strategic decision-making in international affairs, even though human judgement is still crucial.*

12.2. AI as a Diplomatic Strategic Resource

AI serves as a strategic equaliser as well as a capability multiplier in international politics.

12.2.1. Predictive Geopolitics

AI algorithms estimate geopolitical trends by analysing large datasets, including economic flows, military activities, and signs of civil unrest, climatic data, satellite images, and online conversation.

These systems are used by governments to predict the following:

- Diplomatic crises;
- Regime instability;
- Alliance changes;
- The impact of sanctions; and
- The paths of conflict escalation.

AI-driven early warning systems, for instance, are able to detect growing ethnic tensions or economic stress long before they materialise into open violence, allowing for preventive diplomacy as opposed to reactive intervention.

12.2.2. The Art of Negotiation

By examining historical treaty wording, negotiating states' behavioural patterns, power imbalances, and cultural and strategic preferences, advanced models replicate negotiation scenarios.

This enables diplomats to maximise concession frameworks, anticipate red lines, and test negotiation tactics. Strategic calibration takes precedence over guesswork in diplomacy.

12.2.3. Soft Power and Strategic Communication

AI improves public diplomacy as well. Governments use AI to improve cultural and educational diplomacy, monitor global mood, counter negative narratives, and tailor diplomatic messaging to foreign audiences.

Soft power is becoming more and more computational, influenced more by digital perception than by physical presence.

Diagram: AI-Driven Diplomatic Decision-Making Flow

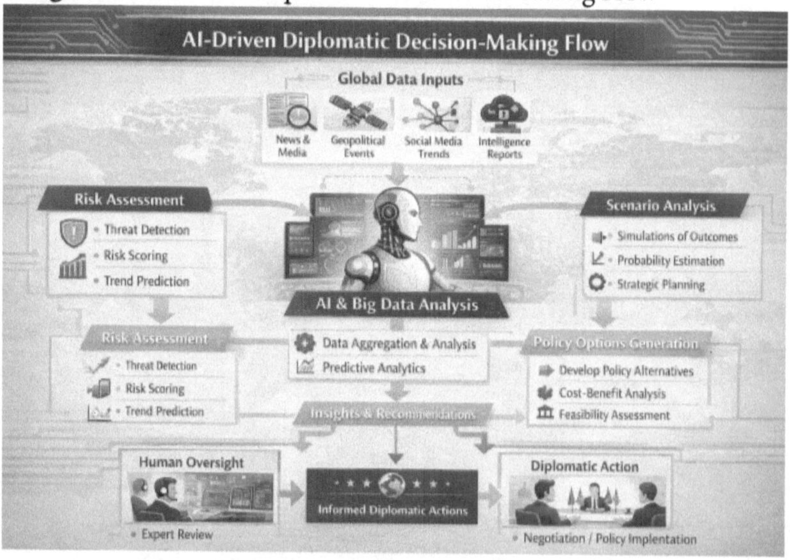

Figure 14: AI-Driven Diplomatic Decision-Making Flow

Figure 14: *The idea of human-in-the-loop diplomacy is reinforced by this figure, which shows how AI serves as a decision-support tool rather than a decision-maker.*

12.3. Global Case Studies of Algorithmic Diplomacy in Action

12.3.1. AI-Powered Statecraft in the United States

The US incorporates AI into strategic messaging, diplomatic forecasting tools, and intelligence fusion centres. AI supports alliance coordination, monitors global instability, evaluates the efficacy of sanctions, and detects foreign influence efforts.

However, there are internal discussions in U.S. diplomacy around ethical deployment, transparency, and the potential for algorithmic bias to impact foreign policy choices.

12.3.2. China: AI as a Tool for Diplomacy

AI is viewed as a vital tool of national power in China. China develops digital dependencies, exports its governance philosophy, and shapes international norms through projects related to digital infrastructure, smart surveillance exports, and AI-driven governance models.

By coordinating technology, trade, and geopolitical influence—especially in the Global South—AI helps China's long-term diplomatic strategy.

12.3.3. Russia: Hybrid Diplomacy with AI

Russia uses AI for strategic signalling, cyber diplomacy, and information warfare. AI is used to support asymmetric diplomatic pressure, amplify influence activities, and analyse societal divisions in competitor states.

Here, AI blurs the distinctions between information operations, coercion, and negotiation as an instrument of hybrid diplomacy.

Diagram: AI-Driven Applications across Diplomatic Functions

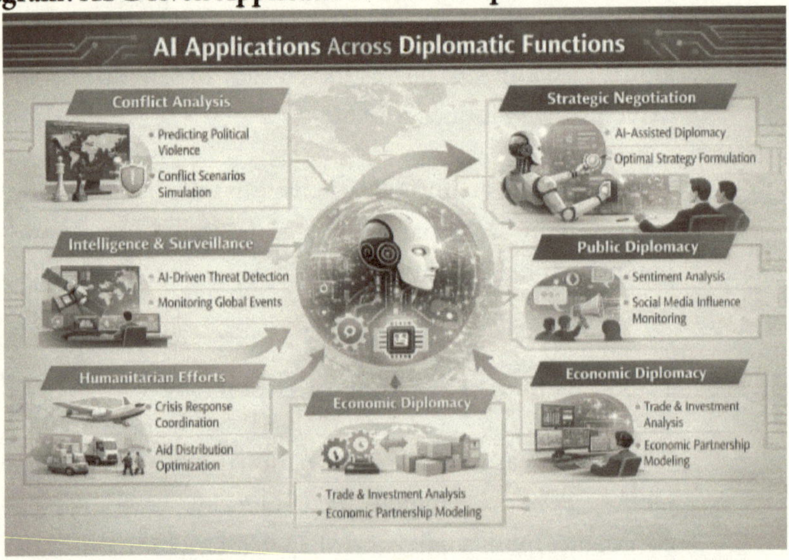

Figure 15: AI-Driven Applications across Diplomatic Functions

***Figure 15:** Outlines the primary areas where AI improves diplomatic ability, including global story management, negotiation optimisation, and crisis prevention.*

12.4. The Global South, AI, and Power Asymmetry

The uneven distribution of power brought about by sophisticated AI and data-driven systems in international relations is known as *Algorithmic Power Asymmetry in Global Diplomacy.*

Diplomatic advantages are disproportionately granted to states and entities having greater access to AI capabilities, big data, computational infrastructure, and algorithmic knowledge. Improved intelligence analysis, political behaviour prediction modelling, automated negotiating support, influence operations, and real-time strategic decision-making are some of these benefits. Because of this, *countries with modern technology are better able to foresee crises, create narratives, and establish global agendas than states with less advanced technology.*

This imbalance runs the risk of exacerbating global inequality, excluding developing nations from meaningful engagement in digital diplomacy, and transferring authority from conventional diplomatic norms to opaque, algorithm-driven procedures. Concerns regarding sovereignty, accountability, transparency, and digital dependency are also raised by the possibility that states without domestic AI capabilities would depend on international platforms that covertly incorporate foreign political objectives.

Computational power asymmetry essentially redefines global power hierarchies in the AI era by turning diplomacy from a contest of alliances and negotiating abilities into a competition over data domination and computational control.

For poor countries, AI presents both opportunities and risks.

12.4.1. **Empowerment through Diplomacy**

Smaller states can benefit from AI by:

- Analysing complicated treaties;
- Managing international talks;
- Identifying exploitative trade terms; and
- Strengthening evidence-based diplomacy.

States with a small diplomatic corps can outperform their peers when they have access to AI capabilities.

12.4.2. Technological Colonialism and Digital Dependency

But depending too much on foreign-owned AI platforms carries the following risks:

- Data sovereignty loss;
- Strategic manipulation; and
- Diplomatic reliance.

National autonomy is jeopardised if algorithms influencing diplomatic decisions are under external control. A new kind of geopolitical subordination is algorithmic reliance.

12.5. The Age of AI and Multilateralism

By changing how governments collaborate, negotiate, and manage common global issues, the Age of AI is redefining multilateralism. By facilitating data-driven policy coordination, pandemic and conflict early warning systems, climate modelling, and real-time treaty compliance monitoring, artificial intelligence improves multilateral institutions. International organisations can transition from reactive diplomacy to anticipatory and preventative governance thanks to these capabilities.

AI also puts additional pressure on multilateralism. While conflicting national AI plans run the risk of dividing global governance, unequal access to AI technologies leads to power imbalances among states. Traditional principles of transparency, inclusivity, and consensus-building that support multilateral organisations are further challenged by algorithmic opacity, bias, and the dominance of private technology companies.

As a result, the Age of AI necessitates a new kind of multilateralism that places an emphasis on ethical norms, shared AI governance frameworks, expanding state capacity building, and common monitoring of cross-border AI systems. Whether AI is used as a tool for international cooperation rather than as a catalyst for digital rivalry and geopolitical division will determine the success of multilateralism in this day and age.

International organisations are finding it difficult to keep up with the diplomatic ramifications of AI.

12.5.1. AI in International Governance

AI is being used more and more by institutions including the United Nations, World Trade Organisation, and African Union for the following purposes:

- Conflict monitoring;
- Humanitarian coordination;
- Climate diplomacy; and
- Policy modelling.

However, governing structures do not keep up with the advancement of technology.

12.5.2. The Struggle for AI Standards

There is a worldwide competition to establish:

- Data governance regulations;
- Military AI limitations;
- Ethical standards; and
- Diplomatic AI transparency.

These discussions represent opposing worldviews, hence they are not impartial. Authoritarian systems place more emphasis on control and stability than liberal democracies do on responsibility and rights. The future balance of power will be shaped by the regulations governing AI diplomacy.

12.6. Algorithmic Diplomacy's Ethical and Strategic Risks

As AI systems increasingly inform or automate foreign policy choices, algorithmic diplomacy poses serious ethical and geopolitical hazards. In terms of ethics, the opacity of algorithms compromises accountability and transparency, making it challenging to defend or challenge diplomatic choices that are impacted by sophisticated or private models. While significant data gathering poses privacy and sovereignty concerns, especially when data crosses borders or is managed by private corporations, bias built in training data can entrench geopolitical stereotypes, marginalise weaker states, and mislead threat assessments.

Strategically, *relying too much on algorithms runs the risk of automation bias, which is the deference of human judgement to machine outputs.* This could escalate disputes based on incorrect signals or forecasts. Additionally, adversarial attacks, data poisoning, and cyber manipulation can target algorithmic systems, transforming diplomatic tools into strategic vulnerability vectors. Furthermore, unequal access to cutting-edge AI capabilities can exacerbate power disparities, upsetting current diplomatic balances and promoting online arms races.

In order to guarantee that algorithmic diplomacy promotes stability rather than erodes confidence and international order, these concerns collectively underscore the necessity of human-in-the-loop decision-making, strong oversight procedures, moral AI standards, and multilateral governance frameworks.

12.6.1. Miscalculation and Bias

Biases in data and design are inherited by AI systems. A faulty model may:

- Misinterpret intentions;
- Increase tensions;
- Strengthen stereotypes; and
- Erode state-to-state trust.

It might be more difficult to identify and fix diplomatic mistakes caused by opaque algorithms.

12.6.2. Wisdom vs. Speed

AI speeds up decision-making, but diplomacy calls for moderation. Quick, automated reactions could:

- **Cause situations** to worsen;
- **Take human judgement** out of delicate discussions;
- **Give over diplomatic agency** to machines is more dangerous than AI per se.

12.6.3. Responsibility and Credibility

Important questions come up when AI affects foreign policy outcomes:

- *Who makes* ***Algorithmic*** *decisions?*
- *How are* ***Mistakes*** *handled?*
- *Are states able to contest* ***Diplomatic moves advised by AI****?*

Trust in international relations declines in the absence of accountability.

12.7. The Future Diplomat: Human-AI Collaboration

The future diplomat will work at the nexus of artificial intelligence and human judgement. By quickly evaluating international data, modelling the results of negotiations, monitoring public opinion, and predicting geopolitical threats, AI will improve diplomacy. Nonetheless, *fundamental diplomatic skills like strategic intuition, trust-building, cultural sensitivity, and ethical reasoning will always be uniquely human.*

Therefore, *human-AI cooperation—where AI acts as a decision-support partner rather than a decision-maker—will be essential to effective diplomacy.* This will allow diplomats to act more quickly, intelligently, and strategically while maintaining human accountability and legitimacy in international affairs.

AI enhances rather than replaces the future diplomat. Combining political judgement, cultural intelligence, ethical reasoning, AI literacy, and strategic foresight is essential for future ambassadors.

In order to ensure that algorithms inform foreign policy rather than dictate it, foreign ministries must invest in AI-competent diplomacy.

12.8. Developing a Structure for Ethical AI Diplomacy

The design and application of AI systems in international relations must incorporate moral responsibility, transparency, and strategic restraint in order to provide a framework for ethical AI diplomacy. Fundamentally, this framework must protect human control over diplomatic choices, guaranteeing that AI serves as a decision-supporting tool rather than an independent actor in issues of international collaboration, war, and peace.

First and foremost, the application of diplomatic AI must be guided by explicit normative principles—fairness, accountability, explainability, respect for sovereignty, and non-discrimination. These values ought to be enshrined in international law and human rights frameworks, as well as institutionalised through multilateral agreements.

Second, strong institutional frameworks are required. This includes mandated impact evaluations for algorithmic tools, auditability standards, safe data governance regulations, and AI ethical review bodies in foreign ministries. It should be common practice to use human-in-the-loop and human-on-the-loop oversight approaches.

Third, inclusive multilateral governance is necessary for ethical AI diplomacy. Preventing algorithmic power imbalances requires clear cross-border data practices, shared technical standards, and capacity building for emerging governments. Global diplomatic AI rules should be coordinated and regulated by international organisations.

In the end, an ethical AI diplomacy framework strengthens collaboration, legitimacy, and stability in the AI-driven international system by converting AI from a source of strategic risk into a tool that builds trust.

Nations must work towards:

1. Human-in-the-loop decision-making.
2. Algorithmic openness in diplomatic systems in order to protect international stability.
3. Global standards for the application of AI.
4. Developing countries' capacity building.
5. Protections for data sovereignty.

Ethical AI diplomacy is a strategic requirement, not an ideal.

12.9. Conclusion: Code, Power, and Global Relations' Future

The syntax of diplomacy is being rewritten by AI. These days, algorithms influence how countries negotiate interests, project power, and identify threats. The world is about to enter a new era in which behaviour is influenced by code, and those who possess both knowledge and insight will increasingly have a diplomatic advantage.

However, *diplomacy is still fundamentally a human endeavour.* It is impossible to automate trust, empathy, self-control, and moral judgement. The difficulty of AI and international diplomacy is not to choose between people and computers, but to make sure that robots uphold rather than subvert humanity's finest diplomatic ideals.

These days, the global stage is algorithmic. Whether world leaders will be astute enough to stay human is the question.

Chapter 13: Prospects for the Future of AI in Politics

13.1. Overview: The Horizon of Algorithms

Politics, government, leadership, diplomacy, and public participation have all changed as a result of artificial intelligence. As the Algorithmic Age draws near, the upcoming ten years will present revolutionary opportunities, previously unheard-of difficulties, and significant concerns over the direction of political power.

Artificial intelligence is no more a theoretical idea in politics; *it is actively influencing public policy, elections, government, and diplomacy all around the world.* AI's trajectory points to an era of "algorithmic politics," when data-driven decision-making coexists with—or even challenges—traditional human political processes, from automated systems that optimise public service delivery to predictive analytics that predict voter behaviour.

"In the Algorithmic Age, human intelligence, morality, and bravery will be the key indicators of leadership rather than the AI's intelligence." – **Patrick Mukosha**

The question now is not if AI will have an impact on politics, but rather how much and how. This chapter examines new developments, revolutionary uses, and possible dangers as AI takes centre stage in international politics.

13.2. AI and the Transformation of Elections

The most obvious setting where AI has started to have a significant impact is elections. Prospects for the future indicate more complex applications:

- **Predictive Voter Analytics**: AI will use behavioural and psychographic data to improve micro-targeting tactics. *In order to predict voter preferences with previously unheard-of accuracy, models will examine social media sentiment, emotional cues, and digital interactions in addition to demographics.*
- **Automated Campaign Messaging**: Real-time speeches, ads, and social media posts catered to particular voter groups will be produced via machine-generated material. *AI has the ability to mimic compelling stories, which might dynamically change public opinion during campaigns.*
- **Electoral Security and Integrity:** AI-powered tools will monitor cybersecurity risks to the country's electoral infrastructure, spot irregularities in voting patterns, and spot disinformation efforts.

Case Study: By simulating voters' propensity to interact with particular policy messaging, AI-driven micro-targeting in the 2024 U.S. presidential elections improved campaign efficiency. By examining multi-platform data streams, emerging technologies in the EU seek to forecast election results weeks prior to polling.

Diagram: AI Electoral Influence Flowchart

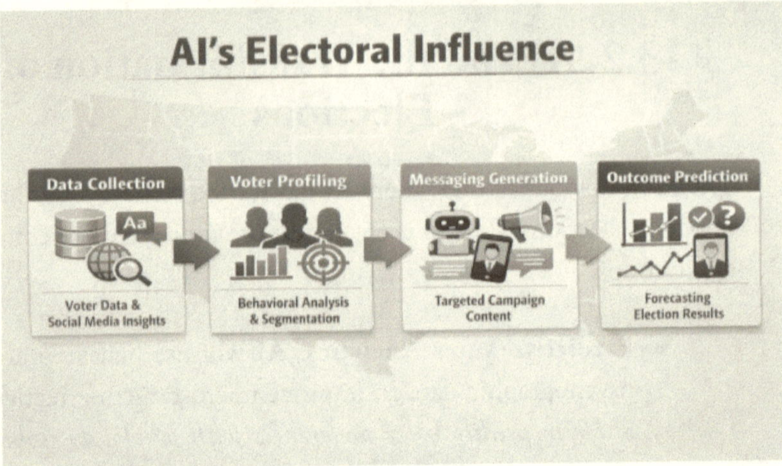

Figure 16: AI Electoral Influence Flowchart

Figure 16: *An illustration of the electoral impact of AI: Data gathering → Voter profiling → Creation of messaging → Prediction of results.*

13.3. AI in Policy Design and Governance

By enabling governments to transition from intuition-based decision-making to evidence-driven, predictive, and adaptive policymaking, artificial intelligence is progressively changing policy formulation and governance. *AI assists policymakers in identifying societal patterns, predicting the effects of policies, and weighing trade-offs prior to implementation through sophisticated data analytics, machine learning, and simulation models.*

AI facilitates scenario modelling, effect assessment, and real-time feedback analysis in policy creation, enabling governments to test various policy choices and make dynamic adjustments. This enhances responsiveness, efficiency, and resource allocation, especially in intricate fields like national security, public health, economic planning, and climate governance.

Through automation, anomaly detection, and performance monitoring, AI improves institutional coordination, service delivery, and regulatory enforcement in governance. But using it also brings up serious issues with algorithmic bias, accountability, transparency, and democratic legitimacy. Inadequately managed AI systems run the possibility of solidifying inequality or transferring authority from democratic institutions to opaque or technocratic systems.

Therefore, in order to ensure that AI enhances rather than diminishes democratic governance, policy legitimacy, and public trust, effective AI-enabled governance necessitates ethical frameworks, legal protections, human monitoring, and public accountability systems.

Governments are increasingly using AI to optimise public policy and administrative efficiency. The trajectory points towards "autonomous governance," where AI helps draft legislation, simulate policy impacts, and monitor regulatory compliance:

- **Predictive Policy Simulations**: Governments can test scenarios before to implementation by using AI to estimate possible effects of policy decisions on economic, social, and environmental variables.
- **Automated Bureaucracy:** AI will expedite routine government procedures, such as tax auditing and licensing, cutting down on human mistake and delays.
- **Citizen Feedback Loops**: In order to inform policy changes almost instantly, AI systems will examine citizen complaints, petitions, and engagement data.

Example: Singapore's Smart Nation effort optimises traffic, utilities, and social programs based on predictive analytics by incorporating citizen feedback into urban planning.

13.4. AI in International Politics and Diplomacy

By altering how states view threats, pursue interests, and interact with one another, artificial intelligence is radically changing international politics and diplomacy. AI improves intelligence collecting, strategic forecasting, negotiation assistance, and diplomatic communication using advanced data analytics, machine learning, and natural language processing, allowing for quicker and better foreign policy judgements.

AI is used in diplomacy to enable early warning systems for conflict, automated treaty monitoring, sentiment analysis of public opinion worldwide, and negotiation outcome simulation. With the use of these instruments, states are able to foresee changes in the geopolitical landscape, proactively handle crises, and maximise diplomatic tactics. But AI also creates algorithmic power imbalances in international relations by favouring entities with more technological capability.

AI challenges established norms of sovereignty and non-interference at the political level by escalating competition through information warfare, influence operations, and cyber-enabled diplomacy. Concerns regarding accountability, escalation risks, and the deterioration of human judgement in crucial international decisions are further raised by the opacity of AI systems.

Diagram: AI in Diplomacy – A Global Monitoring Network

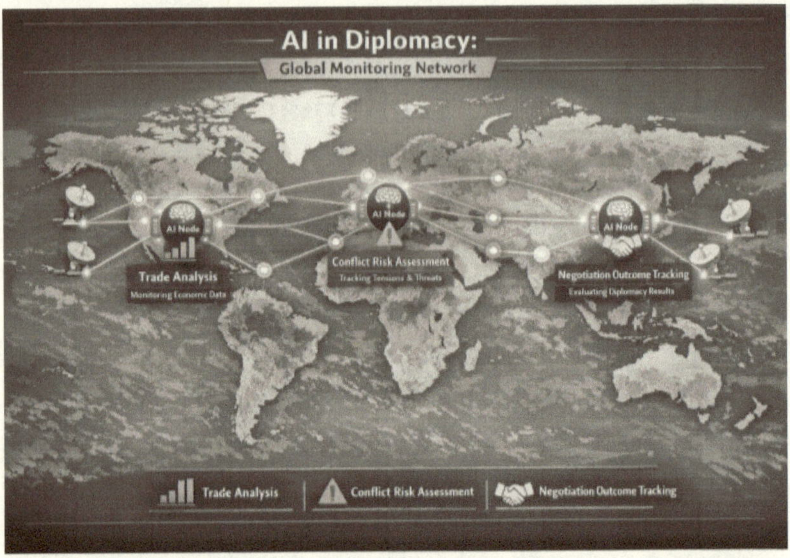

Figure 17: AI in Diplomacy – A Global Monitoring Network

Figure 17: *An Illustration of AI in Diplomacy – where AI nodes monitor conflict risk, trade and negotiation results across the globe.*

A map visualization of AI in diplomacy: AI nodes monitoring trade, conflict risk, and negotiation outcomes across continents.

In order to guarantee that AI acts as a stabilising force rather than a catalyst for geopolitical instability, the incorporation of AI into international politics and diplomacy requires ethical restrictions, human oversight, confidence-building initiatives, and multilateral governance frameworks.

AI will become a strategic instrument in international affairs throughout the next ten years:

- **Predictive Diplomacy:** Proactive diplomatic tactics are made possible by AI's ability to predict probable conflict zones, economic changes, and geopolitical threats.
- **Negotiating and Mediation:** By simulating negotiating situations, AI agents can provide leaders data-driven approaches for trade agreements, peace discussions, or

climate talks.

- **Information Warfare**: Countries will use AI more frequently to keep an eye on their adversaries' online activity, combat misinformation, and carry out influence campaigns worldwide.

Example: China's "AI in Diplomacy" initiative provides policymakers with quick scenario analysis by simulating international treaty outcomes and tracking global economic trends using machine learning algorithms.

13.5. Political Leaders' Cognitive Enhancement

The use of cutting-edge technology and systems, mostly AI-assisted tools, to increase decision-making, strategic thinking, and situational awareness in governance and diplomacy is referred to as political leaders' cognitive enhancement. This improvement typically happens through decision-support technologies, such as AI-driven policy simulations, real-time intelligence analysis, risk forecasting, and scenario modelling, rather than directly modifying the human brain.

With the use of these tools, leaders may better handle massive volumes of information, lessen cognitive overload, foresee the effects of policy decisions, and react to emergencies. Cognitive enhancement can result in quicker, better informed, and more consistent decisions in difficult fields including international diplomacy, economic governance, and national security.

With the use of these tools, leaders may better handle massive volumes of information, lessen cognitive overload, foresee the effects of policy decisions, and react to emergencies. Cognitive enhancement can result in quicker, better informed, and more consistent decisions in difficult fields including international diplomacy, economic governance, and national security.

But there are serious issues with this trend. While unequal access to cognitive-enhancing technology might exacerbate political and geopolitical power imbalances, an over-reliance on AI may erode human judgement, moral reasoning, and responsibility. Transparency, bias, and the validity of decisions influenced by opaque systems are further ethical concerns.

Therefore, the cognitive augmentation of political leaders must continue to be supplemental rather than replacement, based on ethical governance frameworks that uphold democratic scrutiny, human accountability, and confidence in political power.

The application of AI to directly improve political decision-making at the cognitive level is a revolutionary frontier:

- **Brain-Computer Interfaces (BCIs):** When making decisions, future leaders may use AI-integrated BCIs to access real-time data streams, prediction models, and policy simulations.
- **Decision Support Systems:** AI might serve as a digital co-leader by offering moral, financial, and strategic advice while taking long-term societal effects into consideration.
- **Bias Mitigation**: By providing alternate viewpoints based on data-driven analysis, AI may assist leaders in recognising their own cognitive biases.
- **Ethical Consideration**: Although cognitive augmentation might increase productivity and vision, it runs the risk of dividing traditional representatives from "augmented" leaders and possibly consolidating political power in novel, opaque ways.

Diagram: Political Leader Connected to a BCI-AI Network

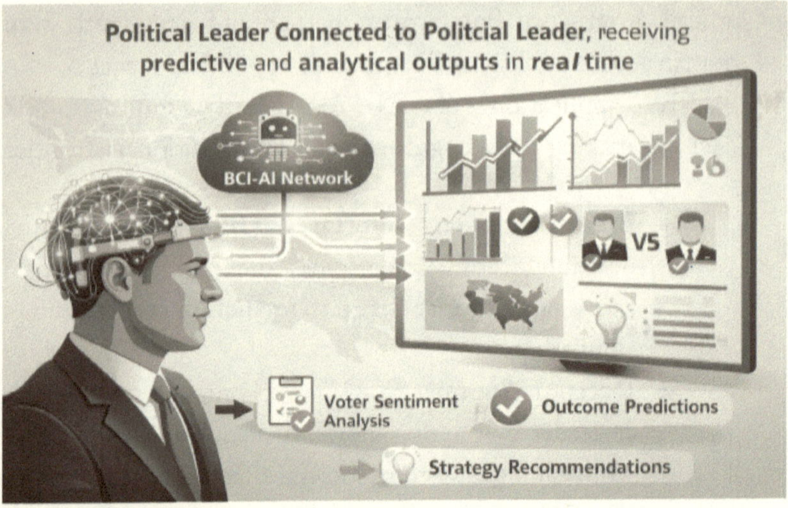

Figure 18: Political Leader Connected to a BCI-AI Network

Figure 18: *An illustration of a political leader linked to a BCI-AI network and obtaining real-time analytical and predictive results.*

13.6. Potential Dangers and Difficulties

There are a number of serious risks and challenges associated with integrating AI into politics, government, and diplomacy. *Over-reliance on AI systems poses a major risk since it might result in automation bias and the deterioration of human judgement in crucial political decisions.* Inaccurate data or models may result in unwise policies or intensify tensions when leaders show undue deference to algorithmic outcomes.

Algorithmic bias and opacity are another significant obstacle. Many AI systems function as "black boxes," making it challenging to defend or explain choices that have an impact on citizens or foreign allies. Biased training data can undermine legitimacy and trust by reinforcing societal injustices, geopolitical biases, or discriminatory policy decisions.

AI also poses threats to sovereignty and security. Governance and diplomatic systems are susceptible to data manipulation, hacks, and foreign meddling. Dependence on outside technology suppliers can limit national autonomy by exposing states to digital reliance.

Lastly, unequal access to AI capabilities exacerbates power disparities both inside and between governments, which could undermine international relations and democratic processes. To ensure that AI enhances governance rather than weakens it, addressing these risks calls for robust ethical frameworks, legal protections, human monitoring, transparency systems, and international cooperation.

Thus, these are risks associated with the use of AI in politics:

1. **Algorithmic Manipulation**: Advanced AI has the potential to influence elections, stifle opposition, and control public opinion.
2. **Opacity and Accountability:** It may be challenging to

assign blame for policy results or ethical transgressions when AI-driven judgements lack transparency.

3. **Global Arms Race**: AI in politics, from automated cyber diplomacy to predictive conflict modelling, may lead to competitive escalations between countries.
4. **Social Divide:** Wealthier countries or elite groups may have unequal access to AI-enhanced political institutions, while others may be marginalised.

Example: As an illustration of how quickly AI might undermine democratic norms if left uncontrolled, consider the use of AI in disinformation operations before elections in several nations.

13.7. Future Scenarios: 2035 and Beyond

Artificial intelligence will become a *structural factor influencing power, legitimacy, and statehood* itself by 2035 and beyond, rather than just a tool for political strategy or governance. *Whether AI strengthens democracy, solidifies digital dictatorship, or compels humanity to completely rethink government will depend on the course societies take now.*

This section presents three likely future scenarios as strategic lenses for political leaders, policymakers, and democratic institutions rather than as forecasts.

Scenario 1: Renaissance of Democratic AI (2035–2050)

- **Summary**

AI is democratically responsible, publicly implemented, and guided by ethics. While maintaining human oversight and public confidence, governments successfully use AI into public administration, elections, and policymaking.

- **Important features include:**
    - Transparent algorithms with public auditability;
    - Strong international standards on ethical AI and digital rights;
    - AI-assisted participatory democracy (digital town halls, deliberative polling); and
    - High citizen AI literacy.
- **Political outcomes include:**
    - Increased democratic legitimacy,
    - Decreased corruption through automated

    - oversight,
    - More responsive, evidence-based governance, and
    - Increased public trust and engagement.
- **Risks include:**
    - Regulatory conservatism has slowed innovation.
    - Oversight and capacity-building are still necessary.
    - Strategic Perspective.

Democracy endures by civilising AI rather than by opposing it.

Scenario 2: Concentration of Algorithmic Power (Digital Authoritarianism)

- **Summary**
  AI turns becomes a tool for mass behavioural manipulation, elite consolidation, and political control. States and businesses that control data, computation, and algorithms gain more power.
- **Important features include**:
    - AI-managed elections with no transparency;
    - Predictive governance and surveillance-driven policymaking;
    - Behaviour score systems influencing service access;
    - The normalisation of deepfake politics and information warfare; and
    - Weak or fragmented global AI regulation.
- **Political Results**
    - Diminished democratic institutions
    - There are elections, but there is no real choice.
    - Algorithmic suppression of political dissent and the reduction of citizens to data subjects
- **Dangers**
    - Social unrest and crises in legitimacy;
    - High susceptibility to systemic AI abuse or

failures; and
- The entrenchment of digital feudalism and inequality
- **Strategic Perspective**:
  - Control without consent results from efficiency without ethics.

Scenario 3: Resetting Post-Democratic Governance (Hybrid Human–AI Systems)

- **Summary**

AI-driven civilisations are too complicated for traditional democratic institutions to handle. Redesigned human supervision mechanisms are combined with AI decision tools to create new hybrid governance models.

- **Important Features include**:
  - Real-time policy proposals from AI systems;
  - Human councils validate or veto algorithmic recommendations;
  - Continuous feedback models replace electoral cycles in governance;
  - AI-mediated international cooperation on climate, health, and security
  - Redefinitions of representation, sovereignty, and legitimacy
- **Political Results**
  - More flexible governance for intricate world issues
  - Decreased mismanagement of crises and policy lag;
  - conflict between efficiency and democratic symbols

- **Risks include**:
    - Cultural opposition to non-traditional government;
    - Ethical ambiguity surrounding AI power;
    - Democratic alienation if humans feel marginalised; and
    - Strategic Perspective.

Democracy may not be abandoned in the future, but it will be rewritten.

Diagram: The Future of Governance - Which Path will we Choose?

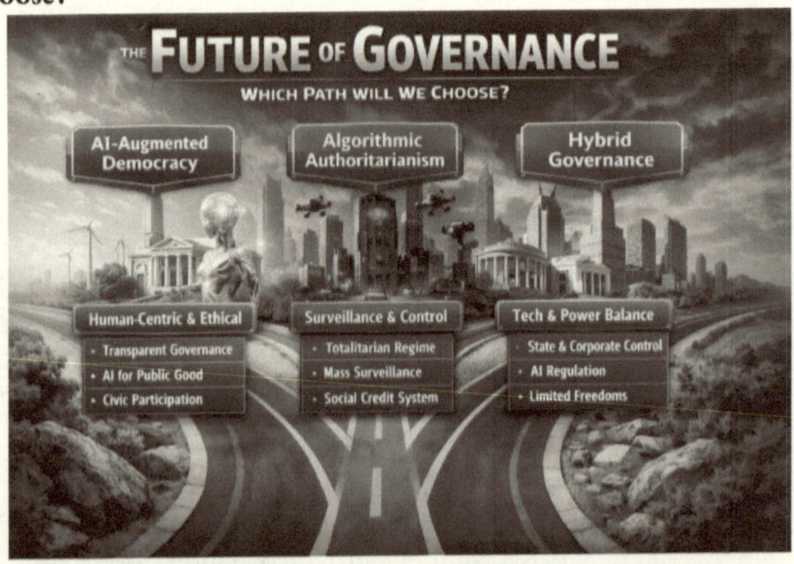

Figure 19: The Future of Governance - Which Path will we Choose?

Figure 19: *A future scenario map with three paths: Algorithmic Dictatorship, Hybrid Government, and AI-Augmented Democracy.*

All Scenarios are Shaped by Cross-Cutting Forces

Regardless of the course chosen, a number of factors will influence governance beyond 2035:

- *Control over data and computing infrastructure;*
- *Public confidence in organisations and technology;*
- *Leaders' and citizens' AI literacy;*
- *International collaboration vs techno-nationalism; and*
- *Moral leadership and political will.*

Whether AI becomes a dictator, a liberator, or a quiet collaborator in government will depend on these factors.

In conclusion, *beyond 2035, governments will be decided politically rather than by technology*. AI has the potential to uphold democratic principles, dangerously consolidate power, or compel a rethinking of political structures. The key question for the post-2035 world is not what AI can accomplish, but rather who controls the algorithms and for whom.

The ability of mankind to stay morally and politically ahead of its technologies will be crucial to democracy's survival in the future.

13.8. Conclusion: Leading the Future of Algorithms

AI is going to completely change politics, from leadership and diplomacy to campaigning and governance. Its course will determine whether countries experience more democratic participation, effective policymaking, and knowledgeable leadership—or encounter power concentration, inequality, and manipulation.

AI is becoming a co-pilot for diplomacy, leadership, and governance rather than a tool.

Its course will impact:

- The speed, precision, and vision of political decision-making;
- The character of democracy and public participation;
- The distribution of power and influence worldwide; and
- The moral underpinnings of 21st-century administration.

Even though politics will be algorithmic in the future, human judgement, morality, and responsibility will still be crucial. Leaders that are adept at fusing human insight with AI will be able to efficiently navigate uncertainty, foresee catastrophes, and serve their constituents.

The question of whether AI will influence politics is no longer relevant in the Algorithmic Age—it has already done so. How leaders will use this authority sensibly, fairly, and responsibly is the true challenge.

It is obvious that citizens, engineers, and legislators must create frameworks that guarantee AI strengthens rather than weakens democratic values. The next political frontier is strategic, ethical, and deeply human in addition to being technology.

Chapter 14: Conclusion - Governing in the Age of Algorithms

As our investigation into AI and politics draws to a close, one thing becomes abundantly evident: *AI is the present, not the future.* AI has already started to change the laws of government, from influencing public opinion to improving leadership cognition, from automating political strategy to redefining diplomacy.

However, results are not determined solely by technology. How people incorporate AI into institutions, political systems, and society is where the real power is found.

"In the Algorithmic Age, leadership is about accountability, vision, and moral stewardship rather than just having access to cutting-edge tools." – **Patrick Mukosha**

Important Lessons

1. **AI as a Political Ally:** AI is an analytical engine, co-creator, and co-strategist. Although it takes human judgement to direct it, it improves human capabilities.
2. **Ethics as a Guiding Principle**: It is impossible to compromise on transparency, justice, accountability, and public confidence. For governance to remain legitimate, ethical AI is crucial.
3. **Resilient Systems Are Crucial**: While AI can improve governance and institutions, resilience calls for human supervision, safe infrastructure, and flexible regulations.
4. **Global Implications**: AI changes international cooperation, trade, diplomacy, and conflict avoidance. AI deployment and literacy will become more crucial to the geopolitical balance of power.
5. **The Human-AI Hybrid Leader**: AI-assisted decision-making, cognitive augmentation, and real-time integration

of public sentiment and policy analytics are all part of the future of leadership. Even as machines become strategic allies, human values continue to be paramount.

Those who listen well, behave morally, and govern sensibly with AI by their side will shape the political landscape of the future. In order to maintain government, citizens must also comprehend and interact with these technologies.

"AI provides an enhanced toolkit, but freedom, justice, and democracy are still exclusively human obligations." – **Patrick Mukosha**

In the Algorithmic Age, human intelligence, morality, and bravery will be the key indicators of leadership rather than the AI's intelligence.

The way forward is obvious: *embrace AI, exercise responsible governance, and make sure that the promise of technology is consistent with human values.*

An Outlook for the Future

The Algorithmic Age offers previously unheard-of opportunities:

- AI can help governments better serve their citizens, anticipate disasters before they happen, and develop evidence-based and insightful policies.
- Leadership may become quicker, better educated, and more inclusive as a result.

However, *when abused, the same technology can undermine democracy, solidify inequality, and sway public opinion.*

The question is not whether AI will alter politics—it has already done so.

Whether World leaders, organisations, and societies will mould AI for the benefit of society is the question.

Table of Figurers

Bibliography

1. *Handbook of Artificial Intelligence and Robotic Process Automation: Policy and Government Applications*[1]. *Anthem Press. 2020. doi*[2]*:10.2307/j.ctv20pxz2v*[3]*. ISBN*[4] *978-1-78527-495-4*[5]*. JSTOR*[6] *j.ctv20pxz2v*[7]*. S2CID*[8] *242891260*[9]*.*

2. *AI used against candidates in this country's election | CNN*[10]*. November 17, 2023. Retrieved 14 August 2025 – via www.cnn.com*[11]*.*

3. *Nicas, Jack; Herrera, Lucia Cholakian (November 16, 2023). Election? "The New York Times. Archived*[12] *from the original on October 8, 2024. Retrieved 13 August 2025.*

4. *Ci, Q. (2025). The Cultural Politics of Artificial Intelligence in China. Theory, Culture & Society, 42(3), 21-40. https://doi.org/10.1177/02632764241304718 (Original work published 2025)*

5. *Dimitriadis, Dimitris (November 15, 2024). "Ghana Becomes the Latest Nation Targeted With AI-generated Election Misinformation"*[13]*. News Guard*[14]*. Retrieved 15 August 2025... using AI to influence elections in Ghana*

---

1. *https://www.jstor.org/stable/j.ctv20pxz2v*
2. *https://en.wikipedia.org/wiki/Doi_(identifier)*
3. *https://doi.org/10.2307%2Fj.ctv20pxz2v*
4. *https://en.wikipedia.org/wiki/ISBN_(identifier)*
5. *https://en.wikipedia.org/wiki/Special:BookSources/978-1-78527-495-4*
6. *https://en.wikipedia.org/wiki/JSTOR_(identifier)*
7. *https://www.jstor.org/stable/j.ctv20pxz2v*
8. *https://en.wikipedia.org/wiki/S2CID_(identifier)*
9. *https://api.semanticscholar.org/CorpusID:242891260*
10. *https://www.cnn.com/videos/world/2023/11/17/exp-argentina-election-artificial-intelligence-pozzebon-pkg-111702pseg2-cnni-world.cnn*
11. *http://www.cnn.com*
12. *https://web.archive.org/web/20241008072527/https:/www.nytimes.com/2023/11/15/world/americas/argentina-election-ai-milei-massa.html*
13. *https://www.newsguardrealitycheck.com/p/ghana-becomes-the-latest-nation-targeted*
14. *https://en.wikipedia.org/wiki/NewsGuard*

6. Swenson, Ali; Chan, Kelvin (March 14, 2024). "Election disinformation takes a big leap with AI being used to deceive worldwide"[15]. Associated Press[16]. Archived[17] from the original on March 18, 2024. Retrieved 13 August 2025.

7. Feliba, David. "How AI shaped Milei's path to Argentina presidency | Context". www.context.news. Archived[18] from the original on May 24, 2024. Retrieved 14 August 2025.

8. "Deepfaked video of broadcast alleges Ukraine tried to assassinate French president"[19]. Wired[20]. February 19, 2024. Archived[21] from the original on October 9, 2024. Retrieved 15 August 2025.

9. https://www.newsweek.com/china-using-artificial-intelligence-help-make-diplomatic-decisions-1048734

10. https://foreignpolicy.com/2023/03/21/ai-artificial-intelligence-diplomacy-negotiations-chatgpt-quantum-computing/

11. "Government by Algorithm: A Review and an Agenda"[22]. Stanford Law School. Retrieved 9 September 2025

12. Kelby, Christopher (2009). "Explaining IT"[23]. Political and Legal Anthropology Review. **32** *(1): 156–160. doi[24]:10.1111/*

---

15. https://apnews.com/article/artificial-intelligence-elections-disinformation-chatgpt-bc283e7426402f0b4baa7df280a4c3fd

16. https://en.wikipedia.org/wiki/Associated_Press

17. https://web.archive.org/web/20240318065952/https:/apnews.com/article/artificial-intelligence-elections-disinformation-chatgpt-bc283e7426402f0b4baa7df280a4c3fd

18. https://web.archive.org/web/20240524211753/https:/www.context.news/ai/how-ai-shaped-mileis-path-to-argentina-presidency

19. https://flo.uri.sh/visualisation/18134407/embed

20. https://en.wikipedia.org/wiki/Wired_(magazine)

21. https://web.archive.org/web/20241009111648/https:/flo.uri.sh/visualisation/18134407/embed

22. https://law.stanford.edu/publications/government-by-algorithm-a-review-and-an-agenda/

23. https://www.jstor.org/stable/24497537

24. https://en.wikipedia.org/wiki/Doi_(identifier)

j.1555-2934.2009.01035.x[25]. *ISSN*[26] *1081-6976*[27]. *JSTOR*[28] *24497537*[29]. *Retrieved 9 September 2025*

13. "Results – General Election 4 July 2024"[30]. *Brighton & Hove City Council. 5 July 2024. Retrieved 9 September 2025*

14. "Albania appoints world's first AI-made minister"[31]. *POLITICO. 2025-09-11. Retrieved 9 September 2025.*

15. Gardner, Allison. "Don't write off government algorithms – responsible AI can produce real benefits"[32]. *The Conversation. Retrieved 9 September 2025*

---

25. *https://doi.org/10.1111%2Fj.1555-2934.2009.01035.x*

26. *https://en.wikipedia.org/wiki/ISSN_(identifier)*

27. *https://search.worldcat.org/issn/1081-6976*

28. *https://en.wikipedia.org/wiki/JSTOR_(identifier)*

29. *https://www.jstor.org/stable/24497537*

30. *https://www.brighton-hove.gov.uk/news/2024/results-general-election-4-july-2024*

31. *https://www.politico.eu/article/albania-apppoints-worlds-first-virtual-minister-edi-rama-diella/*

32. *https://theconversation.com/dont-write-off-government-algorithms-responsible-ai-can-produce-real-benefits-145895*

Don't miss out!

Visit the website below and you can sign up to receive emails whenever Patrick Mukosha publishes a new book. There's no charge and no obligation.

https://books2read.com/r/B-A-HJNZ-MNGXI

BOOKS 2 READ

Connecting independent readers to independent writers.

Did you love *AI in Politics: The Rise of Algorithmic Governance*? Then you should read *AI in Entertainment: The Algorithm behind the Curtain*[33] by Patrick Mukosha!

[34]

Nowadays, entertainment is an algorithm rather than only an art. *Artificial intelligence is subtly transforming the creative industry through everything from immersive video games to viral social media content, from blockbuster movies to top-charting music.*

Patrick Mukosha takes readers behind the scenes in **AI in Entertainment: *The Algorithm behind the Curtain*,** examining how AI is changing the fundamental elements of game creation, music composition, storytelling, and audience interaction.

---

33. https://books2read.com/u/mVy1zl

34. https://books2read.com/u/mVy1zl

Mukosha demonstrates the instruments and methods driving the future generation of entertainment by fusing in-depth technical understanding with understandable explanations.

Mukosha explains what it means to be a "creator" in an era where humans and machines mix their strengths.

This book offers a plan for comprehending the AI-driven revolution that is changing how we produce, consume, and enjoy entertainment, regardless of whether you are a creative professional, a tech enthusiast, or an inquisitive reader.

About the Author

Patrick Mukosha is an ICT & Management Consultant. With 15+ years of IT experience, he's passionate about all things ICT. He also loves to bring ICT down to a level that everyone can understand. His works have been quoted on Academia by Researchers and ICT Practitioners (www.academia.edu). He has a PHD and MBA from AIU, USA, BSc(Hons) ICT, UEA, UK, Dipl, CCT, UK. He's a founder of PatWest Technologies.